BAPTISM
WHY WAIT?

REES BRYANT

Endorsements

Baptism always is a subject that stirs passionate debate. Dr. Bryant has stepped boldly into the fray and has done so with balance and objectivity. His commitment to careful consideration of all aspects of his subject is to be commended. While not everyone will agree with his conclusions, each reader will have been challenged seriously to look again at the full range of Scripture's statements on this. This is must reading.

> Robert Douglas, Ph.D.
> Professor of World Mission and Church Growth
> Director, Chicago Center for Urban Mission
> Lincoln Christian Seminary

Rees Bryant's *Baptism: Why Wait?* is both theologically astute and missiologically relevant. For too long evangelical missions have artificially segmented baptism and conversion by refusing to baptize adults who profess faith in Jesus Christ but are unable to read or recite the catechism. Baptism is thus reduced to a human act rather than a participation in God's grace. Bryant effectively calls us back to the biblical relationship of baptism and conversion.

> Dr. Gailyn Van Rheenen
> Professor of Missions
> Abilene Christian University

Out of an interest in New Testament teaching and in practices in missions, Rees Bryant, casting his net widely, has given a challenging summary of baptismal discussion of the last half of the twentieth century with which he agrees. He places a wholesome emphasis on the place of baptism in conversion and urges that penitent believers be baptized without delaying for additional programs of instruction. While (because of the past history and present popular understanding of the term "sacrament") I am considerably less enthusiastic than Bryant for regarding baptism as the sacrament of conversion, his case for the essentiality of baptism is unanswerable. Many of the counterarguments are kindly refuted. His summary of the meaning of baptism is excellent. In our time when baptismal teaching is being neglected, Bryant's study places a wholesome emphasis.

> Jack P. Lewis
> Professor of Bible
> Harding Graduate School of Religion

Thank God for a book on a topic of long-standing theological controversy that has both conviction and a peace-loving spirit! In this winsome book Dr. Bryant focuses on the role of baptism in Paul's theology of conversion and missionary practice. In developing his understanding of baptism as a sacrament he is patient with the evidence, careful in critiquing differing positions, and helpful in the way he supplies abundant documentation for further research. Christians in the Stone-Campbell Movement are indebted to Dr.

Continued following p. 224

BAPTISM
WHY WAIT?
*Faith's Response
in Conversion*

REES BRYANT

College Press  **Joplin, MO**

Cover Design by Brett Lyerla

Library of Congress Cataloging-in-Publication Data

Bryant, Rees, 1930–
    Baptism, why wait? : faith's response in conversion/Rees
Bryant.
        p.   cm.
    ISBN 0-89900-858-5
    1. Baptism—Biblical teaching.   2. Conversion—Biblical
teaching.   3. Bible. N.T. Epistles of Paul—Criticism, interpretation, etc.   I. Title
BS2655.B34 B79 1999
234'.161—dc21   99-046669
                                                          CIP

DEDICATION

To Patti — my wife, my best friend, my encourager, and my partner in service. She has offered valuable suggestions and critique as well as typing and retyping the manuscript through the many stages of its development. Without her support the task would never have been accomplished. To her I gratefully dedicate this book.

ACKNOWLEDGMENTS

I am deeply grateful to many people who have encouraged me and given me the opportunity to complete this task.

I express sincere appreciation to Dean S. Gilliland, Arthur F. Glasser, and Charles Van Engen, the dissertation committee at Fuller Theological Seminary, who guided the graduate research that led to this work. Their critique and suggestions were indispensable. Special thanks is due to Dean S. Gilliland, my mentor and friend, whose classes and writings were seminal in my studies. As teacher, he gave most generously to me of his time and energy. Now he has written an insightful foreword to this book. I am profoundly grateful. Thanks are also due to the following: Colin Brown who directed my study of the sacraments; Edgar J Elliston who taught me research design; Arthur F. Glasser who directed my studies of hermeneutics and Jewish antecedents of Christian baptism; Paul G. Hiebert who guided my studies in symbolic anthropology; and Donald and Mary McGavran who suggested that someone from the Stone-Campbell Movement should write a Fuller School of World Mission dissertation on the topic of baptism.

Gratitude is also due to all of my colleagues at Lincoln Christian Seminary where I have taught since 1990. The entire faculty have encouraged me in ways too numerous to mention.

Thanks to John Castelein, Robert Douglas, and Walter Zorn for their gracious endorsements of this book. Thanks to John Castelein, Walter Zorn and Jack Cottrell (of Cincinnati Bible Seminary) for careful critiques during final revisions. Thanks also to Wayne Shaw, our seminary dean, who permitted me to teach a lighter load one semester in order to do additional research on baptism.

I am grateful to the editor, John Hunter, who has provided careful guidance and encouragement during the past year since College Press agreed to publish this work.

Despite the efforts of all these good people, the reader may (alas!) find mistakes and errors. For these I take full responsibility.

Finally, above all, I thank our gracious Father in Heaven, who gives all good gifts, for health and strength sufficient to do this work. May what I have written glorify Him.

TABLE OF CONTENTS

PART TWO: PAULINE PERSPECTIVES OF BAPTISM

FOREWORDS

In this book *Baptism: Why Wait?* Dr. Rees Bryant has made a valuable contribution to the exposition of Paul on baptism in his letters. It is a clear expression of the relation between baptism and conversion. The author has spent a long time in this field and has produced a very careful study into the meaning of baptism.

He has rightly explained Paul's exegesis of Romans 6:1-11. There he has shewn that for a convert to be baptised is to die and be raised from death, but Paul has gone on to state that in that experience the convert has been given a new life in union with Christ. He has also clarified for us Paul's statement in his letter to the Colossians in 2:12 that the convert has been buried with Christ in baptism and been raised with Him through faith in the power of God, who raised Christ from the dead.

This led Dr. Bryant to see that Paul saw that baptism was the climax of conversion, therefore there was no necessity for a period of instruction separating baptism from conversion. Hence the title given to this study — *Baptism: Why Wait?* So in this book the writer has made it plain that a person who has heard the gospel and responded to it is forgiven by God and is adopted into His family.

This will be an excellent book to put into the hands of students, pastors and laymen, who will be very grateful to have such a lucid work on their book shelves. It will not only clarify what baptism is but they will be able to preach its meaning.

George Beasley-Murray
M.A., M.Th., Ph.D.

The magnificence and deep meaning of biblical baptism have always held my interest. My life was formed in a strictly Christian environment with ancestors in the Presbyterian clergy. My Wesleyan father and mother were more educated in the Bible and in the teaching of the Bible than many pastors. However, I received two baptisms. I have always wondered how I might defend myself before my own faculty colleagues on the subject of my personal baptism story. Even though I was baptized as an infant, my Greek New Testament studies led me to seek immersion baptism when I was in college. Rebaptism has always been controversial. In fact, I often wished I knew what God would say about a lot of the confusion, misrepresentation and outright perversion that has developed around baptism.

Having made a personal choice to declare my own faith in and acceptance of Jesus as Savior through baptism, I was baffled when I went to Nigeria as a missionary. Baptism in the church there was practiced more as an incentive for new converts to stop drinking, get rid of extra wives, and learn how to read. In general, the discipline leading to baptism was a sort of "finishing school" for those whom church leaders deemed to be "worthy" of church membership. All sorts of barriers could threaten the right to be baptized, and those who were set aside for longer or shorter periods became second-class citizens in the church. There was always a kind of unspoken shame attached to being a noncommunicant (unbaptized) church attender. In a culture like Africa where ritual is everything and the mystical meanings attached to rituals are powerful, the first thing done after baptism was to take communion. This connection of baptism with the Lord's Supper was felt to be essential in a system where recent believers were separated from the "mature" and more "trustworthy" Christians. However, the result was that to be among the baptized was not so much to confess Jesus Christ and salvation through Christ as it was to have a special standing in the new community called the church.

I worked as a missionary in Nigeria for twenty-two years so I am not speaking sarcastically or with disrespect, even though it may sound so. The rationale for delaying baptism and allowing baptism for the selected few was based upon the need to "model" what first generation Christians ought to be. There was the fear, justified in some ways, that a compromise on quality of life would undermine the new church. Little wonder that my African students were amazed that the Apostle Paul would baptize the likes of the Philippian jailer (and his household) or the woman Lydia only hours after their confession of saving faith.

This reality lies in the background as to why, after generations of church dogma and theology, we still need this study by Rees Bryant. Often in planting churches and training leaders in cultures different from their origin, our denominations and mission organizations fear losing something from the distinctives they have stood for. To guard against this, expectations, rules and legal codes are placed on new converts which have little to do with God's grace or the simplicity of saving faith. The meaning of baptism and practices governing baptism become trapped in tests of how much knowledge the believer has and what kind of behavior he or she demonstrates. Judgments as to how the believer "measures up" are made by church leaders (who themselves are sinners, but for the forgiving grace of God through Christ). Rees Bryant makes it abundantly clear that his inquiry into baptism is not something new as far as historical or biblical theology goes. Rather, it is mission practice and the worldwide spread of the gospel that generates a need for this study. What is the role of baptism when looking at today's unparalleled opportunities for witness, especially at the brink of a new millennium?

Coming from the Churches of Christ it is no surprise that Dr. Bryant has an interest in the issue of baptism, especially around the question of its relationship to conversion. He carefully draws from the best of scholarship to show that baptism is not an afterthought or a celebrative rite subsequent to conversion. He speaks of the unity of baptism and conversion in a variety of ways, probably best summed up by his reference to baptism as "the completion of conversion."

Of course, the mystery of spiritual conversion is finally known only to God, for God alone knows the intentions of a repentant sinner and his or her discernment of grace. Yet conversion can never be stated more simply or more profoundly than in Peter's sermon at Pentecost when he said, "Repent, and let everyone of you be baptized in the name of Jesus Christ for the remission of sins; and you shall receive the gift of the Holy Spirit" (Acts 2:38). Repentance and baptism cannot be separated if we are true to the apostolic faith. Tradition, history, theology, creeds or whatever set aside, this is what baptism means if a person is to come under the lordship of Jesus Christ. Bryant never says that baptism brings salvation. Baptism without the *turning* of repentance or confessing the lordship of Jesus does bring shame to the gospel and the church. Baptism is the outward testimony of the human acceptance of the gift of divine grace. It must be kept as a sacramental act that unites a finite sinner with an infinite and forgiving God. As such, baptism cannot become a ploy, a reward, a rite of self-gratification or a superficial symbol of church membership.

As a foundation to his scriptural view of baptism Rees Bryant has given attention to hermeneutical method and has integrated biblical truth with insights from some of the best scholars. He has resisted the temptation to discuss methods of baptism, while being clear about what he feels the biblical terminology calls for. He raises baptism to the level of sacrament without becoming transcendental or magical.

He has done a service to his own church tradition as well as to all who are engaged in the discipling of Christian believers whether in North America or in other world cultures.

I know the writer of this book as a biblical scholar, servant of the church, missionary and brother in the Lord. What he has written comes from a mission heart with intense convictions. I am sure this comprehensive study comes from Dr.

Bryant as a gift to all who love the Word and are committed to the spreading of the gospel of our Lord and Savior Jesus Christ worldwide.

> Dean S. Gilliland
> M.A., M.Th., Ph.D.
> Senior Professor of Contextualized
>   Theology and African Studies
> School of World Mission
> Fuller Theological Seminary

PREFACE

This is a descriptive study. Although historical investigation is included, this work is not basically an historical study. Although there is a strong theological emphasis, this is not exclusively a theological study. Rather, it might best be characterized as theological missiology. It is not written merely to the academic community, but also to ministers, teachers, and to the world mission leadership community with the hope that it will be helpful to them and to those they serve in the task of world evangelization.

I have quoted extensively from the writings of G.R. Beasley-Murray, Jack W. Cottrell, and Dean S. Gilliland because they say so well what needs to be said. Beasley-Murray has, in my opinion, written the definitive twentieth-century book on baptism. My debt to him cannot be measured. In the Stone-Campbell Movement, no writer has been more helpful to me on this topic than Cottrell. He has written extensively and carefully on baptism. My debt to him is great indeed. As mentioned in the acknowledgments, the writings of Gilliland have been seminal to my studies, both of missions in general and of baptism in particular. I urge the reader to pay careful attention to all the writers I have quoted, but especially to Beasley-Murray, Cottrell, and Gilliland.

Rees Bryant, D.Miss.
Professor of World Mission
Lincoln Christian Seminary
Lincoln, Illinois
August 1, 1999

Chapter I

INTRODUCTION

In a class at the Fuller Theological Seminary School of World Mission an Anglican bishop from Uganda asked, "Was Paul's conversion complete on the Damascus road or was it complete when Ananias baptized him?" The professor replied, "What do you think?" To which the student responded, "If I knew the answer, I would not be asking the professor!" All of us in the class burst out laughing, but we all knew that an important question had been asked. During the following class session, the professor, Dean S. Gilliland, treated seriously the issue of the role of baptism in Pauline theology of conversion, and he later wrote that "baptism is central to our understanding of conversion" (1983:91).

What Is the Role of Baptism?

Yes. But what, precisely, is the role of baptism in Paul's theology of conversion? In Pauline theology, is baptism a part of conversion or does conversion come first and baptism later? Is baptism "almost part of the experience of saving faith" (Gilliland 1983:90) or is baptism an expression or embodiment of saving faith?

If baptism has a place in Paul's theology of conversion, is it the point at which the new convert is incorporated into Christ and into His spiritual body, the church? Is it the occasion during which saving faith receives what grace gives? Is baptism, for the new convert, the end of his old life of sin and the beginning of his new life in Christ? Does baptism complete conversion? Or does baptism have no role in Pauline theology of conversion? Is it merely symbolic of a previous, already-completed conversion experience?

Is there a Biblical urgency to baptism? Is baptism a sacrament? Or is it merely an external rite which can be delayed for various reasons? Does calling baptism an ordinance settle these questions? Should baptism take place only after a period of instruction following saving faith and repentance? Should it take place only after acceptance of a church's creedal statement? Should baptism take place only after ecclesiastical examination of the candidate's motives or personal commitment?

Should baptism be a part of the conversion experience regardless of the culture of the convert? Is conversion best seen as a process which both precedes and follows an encounter/decision? Was "the baptism of new converts in Paul's ministry . . . so much a part of the faith encounter that conversion and baptism could not be separated" (Gilliland 1979:16)?

A Search for Answers

These, and similar questions, though quite controversial among modern theologians, missionaries, and ministers, will be answered in this book. Answers to these questions will be found by an examination of the role of baptism in Paul's conversion, in his theology, and in his missionary ministry. Specifically, I shall address the following questions:

Baptism in Paul's Conversion

What was the role of baptism in the conversion of Paul? Did baptism play any part at all in Paul's conversion? Was

Paul's baptism merely symbolic of a conversion which was complete without it on the Damascus road? Why was Paul's baptism something that Ananias told him he must do without waiting (Acts 22:16)?

Baptism in Paul's Theology

What was the role of baptism in the theology or teaching of Paul? G.R. Beasley-Murray found baptism in sixteen passages written by Paul (1962:vii,viii). What light do these passages cast on our topic?

Baptism in Paul's Ministry

What was the role of baptism in Paul's missionary ministry? Did Paul and his missionary companions baptize new converts as a part of conversion? In Paul's missionary ministry, was baptism the point at which new converts were clothed with Christ and incorporated into His church? Was there an urgency which Paul's ministry connected to baptism? Or, in Paul's missionary ministry, were new believers baptized only after delays for additional teaching, for examination of their motives, or for similar reasons? What light does Paul's ministry cast on his theology of conversion?

Definitions

The following basic definitions of key words and terms should be considered before we proceed:

Baptism

According to the *Hamlyn Encyclopedic World Dictionary*, baptism is "a ceremonial immersion in water, or application of water, as an initiatory rite or sacrament of the Christian church" (1979:154). This, no doubt, is the essence of the meaning of the word in current English usage. However, Arndt and Gingrich define the Greek word, βαπτίζω (*baptizo*), as follows:

> *Dip, immerse, . . . dip oneself, wash* (in non-Christian lit. also 'plunge, sink, drench, overwhelm'), . . . As the Christian sacrament of initiation after Jesus' death Ac 2:41; 8:12f,36,38; 16:33; 22:16; I Cor 1:14-17; D7 (where baptism by pouring is allowed in cases of necessity) . . . (1979:131).

But, since "D=Didache" in Arndt and Gingrich, "baptism by pouring . . . in cases of necessity" is a post-New Testament meaning which differs from Pauline usage. According to Kittel, βάπτω (*bapto*) means "to dip in or under" and *baptizo* "occurs in the sense of 'to immerse' . . . from the time of Hippocrates, in Plato and esp. in later writers" (1964:529-530).

Accordingly, I shall not include a discussion of the mode of baptism as a part of this book. Instead, I shall accept the meaning which Arndt and Gingrich and Kittel give to the word. I shall define baptism as immersion and Christian baptism as a "ceremonial immersion in water . . . an initiatory rite or sacrament of the Christian church."

Conversion

William Barclay has stated that "the basic idea [in conversion] is that of a turn, a change of direction, a reversal of life" (1963:25). According to Stephen Smalley, "conversion is a turning to God *through* commitment to Christ" (1964a:220). Hans Kasdorf wrote that conversion "means to be turned, changed, transformed, renewed, reborn, reconciled, and restored; it is a process which affects the total life-way of the convert" (1980:25). Edmund Gibbs asserts that "in the Christian usage of the term, conversion is one way of describing the individual's initial turning to Christ. It underscores the fact that such a turning is understood as a complete about-face rather than a minor course-correction in the pathway of life" (1986:1).

Although this work will be informed by these definitions and by a continued investigation of Paul's conversion, theology, and ministry, I shall define conversion as a believer's initial turning to God through Jesus Christ. Even though a believer's later turnings to God may be so regarded as to view the whole Christian walk as a life-long conversion process, I shall not use the word conversion in such a broad and unusual sense. Instead, I shall use conversion in its more widely recognized sense as an initial turning to God and consider whether baptism in Paul's conversion, theology, and ministry had a part in that turning.

Pauline Theology

George Ladd points out that "Paul's letters are not theological treatises nor formal literary productions but 'unliterary,' living, personal correspondence, written with deep feeling to Christian congregations that for the most part Paul himself had brought into being" (1974:376). In his epistles Paul was not writing systematic theology. Instead, he was usually writing contextual theology by responding to urgent needs or problems among the newly-established churches. For example, his teachings on baptism in Romans 6:1-4, Galatians 3:26-27, and Colossians 2:11-14 were occasioned by needs of the Christians in Rome, Galatia, and Colosse.

Still, even though Paul's New Testament epistles are not systematic theology, they do contain, together with his teachings in Acts, so far as we know, the only teachings of Paul still in existence on any subject. Hence, I shall turn to them for an authoritative statement of the role of baptism in Pauline theology of conversion.

To present all the issues related to baptism in general is beyond the scope of this book. For example, as I investigate this topic, I have chosen to examine neither the mode of baptism nor infant baptism.

Issues Not Addressed

Although a study of the mode of baptism would be quite interesting, I do not intend to discuss whether immersion or sprinkling is the proper form of baptism. Instead, as mentioned above, I shall accept the authority of Arndt and Gingrich and Kittel that *baptizo* and *bapto* mean immersion in the Greek New Testament. Since any other understanding of baptism was apparently a post-New Testament understanding of it, such is beyond the scope of my investigation of the place of baptism in *Pauline* theology.

With regard to infant baptism, I accept the authority of Paul K. Jewett who studied the relevant patristic material and found that the "earliest express mention of infant baptism in the history of the church" was in a treatise written by Tertullian "between A.D. 200 and 206" (1978:20-21). In view of this finding and in view of there being no clear New Testament mention of infant baptism, it is beyond the limits of this study to investigate the question. Furthermore, the topic of infant baptism is outside the scope of *conversion* which is a major emphasis of this work.[1]

Purpose

It is a major purpose of this work to consider whether baptism had a role in Pauline theology of conversion and, if so, to consider what that role was. It is also an important purpose of this book to determine whether baptism should be regarded as a part of conversion to Christ today or whether it should take place only after the new believer's conversion and a subsequent delay for further instruction, acceptance of a church's creedal statement, or an ecclesiastical examination of a candidate's motives.

Methodology

But studying such issues involves the use of a method of investigation. What methodology should be used?

I take a high view of the inspiration and the authority of the Bible as the word of God. I concur with the Fuller Theological Seminary Statement of Faith:

> All the books of the Old and New Testaments, given by divine inspiration, are the written word of God, the only infallible rule of faith and practice. They are to be interpreted according to their context and purpose and in reverent obedience to the Lord who speaks through them in living power (1986:9).

But to say that the Old and New Testaments "are to be interpreted" raises the issue of Biblical hermeneutics, an issue that must be raised when anyone goes beyond merely *reading* the words of the Biblical texts and asks about the *meaning* of those words. Going beyond mere reading and asking about the meaning of Biblical texts involves one in an explanatory process usually described by the three terms "interpretation," "exegesis," and "hermeneutics." Although there is some overlapping among these words and a lack of precise usage of them in theological and Biblical studies areas, I regard the following definitions by Don McGaughey as adequate for this study:

> INTERPRETATION: Interpretation is the general term implying or including both terms exegesis and hermeneutics. Interpretation is the finished product of the complete exegetical and hermeneutical processes.
> EXEGESIS: Exegesis is the fruit of primary inquiry into a text. Exegesis is the meaning of the text. It takes into consideration such problems as text, date, authorship, purpose, historical background, contextual situation, semantics and linguistics in general. . . .
> HERMENEUTICS: Hermeneutics takes up the process of interpretation where exegesis concludes. Hermeneutics seeks to appropriate the results of an exegetical inquiry. It seeks to make relevant the meaning that exegetical inquiry has discovered. Technically hermeneutics is not the process of appropriation; it is rather the principles upon which the appropriation is accomplished. . . . When used in reference

to the Bible then, hermeneutics may be defined as the science of making the Biblical documents relevant to contemporary man (1960,61:252-253).

While a survey of the various schools of New Testament interpretation throughout the history of the church lies beyond the scope of this study, it is necessary to recognize that there has been a wide diversity of hermeneutical methodologies. A listing of some of the major methodologies indicates to some degree the extent of that diversity.

Some Earlier Hermeneutics

Origen of Alexandria and Caesarea (185-254) tried to solve the historical problems in the Gospels by the allegorical method.[2] Over against him were Theodore (350-428) and Chrysostom (347-407) of Antioch who represented the literal-historical school of interpretation.[3] Although the allegorical method prevailed during the Middle Ages, especially in the work of Gregory the Great (540-604), its search for "deeper meanings" or for "spiritual senses" of Scripture was held in check by a dogmatic hermeneutic which stressed that all interpretation should agree with the body of accepted church doctrine.[4] Martin Luther rejected both the allegorical and the dogmatic methods to insist on accepting the plain and literal meaning of Scripture (F.F. Bruce 1977:31).[5] John Calvin also repudiated the time-honored allegorical method and the dogmatic method as well, even to the extent of doing Biblical exegesis which disagreed with his own *Institutio*.[6]

Contemporary Hermeneutics

The two most widely used hermeneutical methodologies on the contemporary scene are the grammatico-historical and the historical-critical methods. Although I do not regard either of these as a "divine hermeneutic," the following discussions of each of them will present the continuing diversity in this area of New Testament studies and will also give reasons for my choosing the former rather than the latter.

The Grammatico-Historical Method

The desire to avoid the subjectivism of allegorical methods and the dogmatism and foregone conclusions of theological systems led not only Luther and Calvin but also a host of post-Reformation exegetes such as Charles Hodge (1797-1878), H.A.W. Meyer (1800-73), I.H. Marshall, and Ralph P. Martin to adopt the grammatico-historical method. Martin puts his case for this method succinctly in the following words:

> The grammatico-historical method has everything to commend it as an antidote to both of the approaches mentioned. It takes seriously God's revelation which he has been pleased to communicate in verbal form in the pages of holy Scripture. . . . For that reason, the reader begins his enquiry into the meaning of a passage with a conscious endeavour to know what the words (Gr. *grammata*) meant in their historical setting. And that means that he will strive to gain understanding of the text through the language-form which any specific passage employs (1977:222).

According to Martin, certain corollaries follow from this approach:

> The student will want to satisfy himself, as far as he is able, that either the Greek Testament in front of him or the translation based upon it is the "best." By that word is meant that it is as close to the original autographs as it is possible to get through the science of textual criticism. . . .
>
> The other matter is the ascertaining of the meaning of the Greek words and their translation equivalents in our native language. For this we need the help of grammar books, lexicons, dictionaries and concordances. . . .
>
> Then, the clothing of God's saving revelation of himself in historical events and their interpretation means that the

present-day student must take history seriously and be alive
to the setting of Scripture's story as far as the New Testament is concerned in the world of first century Graeco-
Roman society. . . .

Furthermore, the grammatico-historical method enters a
needed protest against an inordinate desire for relevance
which marks out the impressionistic approach (1977:222).

The Historical-Critical Method

The historical-critical method is a serious rival to the grammatico-historical approach to Biblical interpretation. Growing
out of the eighteenth-century Enlightenment and based on
rationalistic presuppositions, the historical-critical method has
been used by such scholars as J.J. Griesbach (1745-1812),
F.D.E. Schleiermacher (1768-1834), F.C. Baur (1792-1860),
Albert Schweitzer, Rudolf Bultmann and many others. Ladd
credits this approach with the following important contributions
to New Testament interpretation: (1) an earlier, more accurate
text of the New Testament; (2) an improved knowledge of *koine*
Greek; (3) an understanding that the Gospels were a literary
form; (4) the discovery of many points of contact between the
New Testament and its historical environment; (5) improved
word studies of New Testament Greek; and (6) important
archaeological discoveries (1967:52). Nevertheless, he rejects it
in favor of what he calls an "historical-theological methodology" (1967:14). Ladd reasons as follows:

> It has become quite clear that neither the historical-critical
> method as it arose in German scholarship and was trans-
> planted to America, nor the liberal theology that often
> accompanied it, was the product of a truly objective study
> of the Bible. . . . It has also become clear that the histori-
> cal-critical method itself did not emerge as the result of
> open-minded, neutral, objective study of the Bible, but was
> motivated by rationalistic presuppositions which had no
> room for the biblical claim to revelation and inspiration
> (1967:10).

According to E. Earle Ellis, "our modern historical-critical method . . . is deficient: although it can show certain interpretations to be wrong, it can achieve an agreed interpretation for virtually no biblical passage" (1977:209).

The method, as it has been used in search for the "historical Jesus," actually caused Bultmann to conclude: "I do indeed think that we can now know almost nothing concerning the life and personality of Jesus" (Ladd 1967:186). With reference to Bultmann's assertion that there is no personality of Jesus in the New Testament, C.S. Lewis asks, "Through what strange process has this learned German gone in order to make himself blind to what all men except him see? What evidence have we that he would recognize a personality if it were there? For it is Bultmann *contra mundum*" (1967:156). Speaking of such scholars as Bultmann, Lewis states that the authority of experts in this methodology would press us "to give up a huge mass of beliefs shared in common by the early Church, the Fathers, the Middle Ages, the Reformers, and even the nineteenth century" (1967:153). Lewis also warns us that this approach often involves

> the claim that the real behaviour and purpose and teaching of Christ came very rapidly to be misunderstood and misrepresented by His followers, and has been recovered or exhumed only by modern scholars. . . . The idea that any man or writer should be opaque to those who lived in the same culture, spoke the same language, shared the same habitual imagery and unconscious assumptions, and yet be transparent to those who have none of these advantages, is in my opinion preposterous. There is an *a priori* improbability in it which almost no argument and no evidence could counterbalance (1967:157-158).

Lewis also doubts the liberal historical-critical approach because he finds "in those theologians a constant use of the principle that the miraculous does not occur" and because their consequent attempts to "reconstruct" the "whole *Sitz im Leben*" of ancient texts are only subjectively conceived (1967:158).

My Hermeneutical Approach

Though each of these hermeneutical approaches is a human approach, I believe that the only one consistent with my view of Scripture as the infallible word of God, and with my desire to be as objective as possible in my Biblical studies, is the grammatico-historical method. As I study the questions raised by this topic, I want to know what the words of Scripture meant in their historical contexts. I want to know what God is communicating in verbal form on the pages of His revelation. I desire neither to "reconstruct" nor to "deconstruct" what I read in the books of either the Old or the New Testament. Accordingly, I shall use the grammatico-historical method to investigate the issues studied in this work.

Using this methodology does not imply that I am a mere neutral observer, nor that I am approaching this work with "scientific detachment" or total objectivity. Instead, I care deeply about this topic, the texts I will examine, the issues to be studied, and Him to whom it all relates. From the days when Barton W. Stone, Thomas and Alexander Campbell, and others led a nineteenth century unity movement in America out of which the *a cappella* Churches of Christ and the Christian Churches/Churches of Christ have grown, we who belong to these fellowships have stressed the importance of baptism. Most of our current leaders would agree with Gilliland that "baptism is central to our understanding of conversion" and that "withholding baptism from new believers is an unbiblical practice" (1983:91). Roland Allen opposed a long period of probation for new believers. I think he was right. Allen wrote:

> We have also run a great risk of confusing the minds of the converts as to the true meaning and nature of baptism. . . . we have taught them that the one great need of men is Christ, and that without Christ men cannot attain to righteousness, and then [by delaying baptism] that they must attain to righteousness by themselves in order to receive Christ (1912:96,97).

However, even though most current leaders in the Christian Churches/Churches of Christ and the *a cappella* Churches of Christ agree with Allen and Gilliland and stress the importance of baptism in conversion, we are, as Allan J. McNicol points out,

> in an era in which some Churches of Christ are tempted to embrace many of the trappings of generic Evangelicalism in order to be in solidarity with a larger number of Christians in the wider ecumenical community [and] there has been a tendency to downplay the centrality of our witness on baptism (1994:36).

This tendency to "downplay" baptism is of great concern to me.

As a missionary I was also concerned about the confusion over baptism in Nigeria. Most Protestant missionaries there, and the Africans they had taught, regarded baptism as merely symbolic of an already completed conversion process. Many Nigerian churches taught that baptism should take place only after acceptance of their creedal statements or examination of the candidate's motives by ecclesiastical authorities.

The International Church of Christ, a "discipling movement" which has grown out of the *a cappella* Churches of Christ, baptizes only after "they are convinced that the person really believes and has fully repented and is totally committed" (Flavil R. Yeakley 1988:61). In this movement, candidates are often required to have a "disciple's heart" before baptism; and this evaluation is made, not by the candidate, but by someone else. This I take to be a serious misunderstanding of Pauline teaching and practice with reference to the role of baptism in conversion.

Thus, I approach this study from the perspective of one who stresses the importance of baptism as crucial to understanding conversion and who regrets the wide-spread theologies and practices which minimize and delay baptism for new believers.

Notes

1. For further study of infant baptism, see the following works:

Karl Barth, *The Teaching of the Church Regarding Baptism* (London: SCM Press, 1948).

Oscar Cullman, *Baptism in the New Testament* (London: SCM Press, 1950).

Pierre Charles Marcel, *The Biblical Doctrine of Infant Baptism* (London: James Clarke & Co., 1953).

John Murray, *Christian Baptism* (Philadelphia: Orthodox Presbyterian Church, 1952).

G.R. Beasley-Murray, *Baptism in the New Testament* (London: Macmillan & Co., 1962).

Paul K. Jewett, *Infant Baptism and the Covenant of Grace* (Grand Rapids, Michigan: Eerdmans, 1978).

2. Origen, for example, found it difficult to determine, from John and the Synoptics, whether Jesus cleansed the temple at an early stage of His ministry or towards the end. He used the allegorical method to resolve this problem. F.F. Bruce explained Origen's reasoning as follows:

If the temple is the soul skilled in reason, to which Jesus ascends from Capernaum, a region of less dignity, so as to purify it from irrational tendencies which still adhere to it, then the improbabilities of the literal accounts disappear and the discrepancies between them become irrelevant.

Similarly, when he deals with Jesus' entry into Jerusalem, he interprets Jesus as the word of God entering the soul (which is called Jerusalem). The ass which the disciples loose is the Old Testament properly interpreted; the colt . . . is the New Testament. The statement that no one had ever sat on it is a reference to those who never submitted to the divine message before the coming of Jesus. This treatment of the record is what we nowadays call demythologization, for Origen regards the literal sense as not only inadequate but as downright unacceptable (1977:25-26).

Although Origen and others who used the allegorical method were able on occasions to see "deeper meanings" in Scripture, the method itself, as illustrated above, seems flawed since such a method could permit the text to mean most anything the interpreter wanted it to mean.

3. F.F. Bruce comments on Theodore's methodology:

Theodore treats the Gospel narratives factually: he pays attention to the particles of transition and to the minutiae of grammar and punctuation. He shows some skill in assessing the value of dubious readings and in bringing out the point of a discourse or parable. . . . he had, for his time, an uncommon appreciation of the principles of exegesis (1977:26-27).

Bruce also notes that, for the Antiochene exegetes, the "literal sense was primary, and it was from it that moral lessons should be drawn; the typological [showing the relation between the old and new covenants] and allegorical senses, while not excluded, were secondary" (1977:26).

4. Larry Chouinard points out that "exegesis was largely an effort to assure that interpretation of Scripture squared with the tradition of the church" (1986:200). But toward the end of the Middle Ages the allegorical method declined, and, under the influence of Aristotelian metaphysics, Thomas Aquinas (1225-1274) and other scholastic theologians "elevated the literal and historical over the symbolic" meanings in Biblical interpretation (1986: 201). Nicholas of Lyra (d.1340) was also concerned "to expound the literal sense of Scripture, over against the allegorical. His exegetical emphasis greatly influenced Luther and opened the door for a new wave of interpreters, the Reformers" (1986:201).

5. However, Luther's "Christological" interpretation led him to a "canon within a canon" as depicted in the preface to his Commentary on James where he ventured to write: "What does not teach Christ is not apostolic, even though St. Peter or Paul taught it; again what preaches Christ would be apostolic even though Judas, Annas, Pilate and Herod did it" (Chouinard 1986:202).

6. Calvin's approach is regarded as more "objective" than Luther's. Of it, F.F. Bruce commented:

> Such examples indicate that Calvin the exegete sat quite loose to certain ideas which have come traditionally to be regarded as characteristically "Calvinistic."
>
> In fact, the more objectively grammatico-historical biblical exegesis is, the more widely is it acceptable, whereas exegesis which is controlled by theological *parti-pris* will be appreciated only where the theological outlook is found congenial (1977:33).

Part One

BACKGROUND STUDIES

Chapter II

CONVERSION

As we approach this study of the role of baptism in Pauline theology of conversion, we should attempt, in the first place, to have as clear an understanding as possible of conversion. What is Christian conversion? Is it a sudden, dramatic event or may it be a more gradual process? How does human responsibility relate to God's initiative in conversion? What does the convert turn from and to? What are the inward and what are the outward aspects of Christian conversion? Are there aspects of Christian conversion that are normative regardless of the convert's culture? If conversion is "a believer's initial turning to God through Jesus Christ" as I previously defined it, is there a point in the "initial turning to God" at which we may say that the conversion is complete?

To begin with, it should be acknowledged that the "actual word conversion appears rarely in our English Bible" (D.J. Price 1979:286). But, even though the actual word is rare, the concept it expresses is not. Instead, the word conversion covers a concept which is found frequently in Scripture. Stephen Neill sees conversion as so significant that he wrote, "no other word has been found which so well expresses something essential to New Testament theology" (1978:205). Since the *word* conversion occurs so seldom in Scripture, we cannot have an adequate understanding of conversion by a mere study of the *word* itself. But, since the *concept* of conversion is so frequent and significant in Scripture, we can study the reality of conversion by studying its function as well as by looking at words which describe it. Price puts it this way:

> There is . . . in both Old and New Testament Scriptures, a central life experience recorded repeatedly of turning away from sin and idols to serve the living God. The reality of the conversion event is present in Scripture, even although [sic] there is no one special word used for it. This fact actually points to the depth of the meaning of Christian conversion. *There is no one word for it, because no one word can embrace its comprehensiveness sufficiently!* . . . Our approach to Scripture must therefore look at words, but in partnership with the function of conversion itself as we see it described in the life experience of the people of God (1979: 286-287).

As we now turn to Scripture to better understand conversion, I shall follow the outlines of Smalley (1964a:215) and Price (1979:288) as I take into account the *language* of conversion, then its *illustrations* and finally its *theology* in both the Old and New Testaments. The major headings for this study, "Light from the Old Testament" and "The New Testament Unfolding of Conversion Concepts" are chapter titles from the book *Christian Conversion in Context* by Kasdorf (1980: 37,47).

Light from the Old Testament

The Biblical concept of conversion has very deep Old Testament rootage. From the Fall to the Incarnation, the story of salvation history repeatedly presents the theme of human alienation from God and of God's invitation to a return, to a conversion.

Old Testament Language of Conversion

There appears to be general agreement among recognized scholars that "the deepest roots of the concept of conversion in the Old Testament center in the Hebrew word שׁוּב [*shuv*]" (Price 1979:288). According to *A New Concordance of the Old Testament*, edited by Abraham Even-Shoshan, this verb occurs 1059 times in the Old Testament text (1990:1123).

The word *shuv* does not, however, have a meaning which is inherently sacred or religious. Instead, it is like the English words "conversion" or "convert" which have a broad range of meanings in various life contexts. According to the *Hamlyn Encyclopedic World Dictionary*, it is good English usage for "conversion" to be used in the following nonsacred areas: mathematics, logic, law, sports, psychology and physics (1979: 364). We frequently speak of converting grams into ounces, dollars into pounds or miles into kilometers. Just so, *shuv* is used in a secular sense in the Old Testament:

> [It] describes the action of Reuben, who *returned* to the pit in Dothan to discover Joseph's disappearance (Gen 37:29); or Moses, when he *turned again* into the camp of Israel from the tent of meeting (Ex 33:11). Isaiah uses it to speak of *repulsing* or *turning back* the Assyrian army (Is 36:9) (Price 1979:288).

Basically, then, the Hebrew verb *shuv* refers to a "turning" in the opposite direction.

However, as Price points out, this ordinary word *shuv* came to be used in a special religious or spiritual sense:

> On about 118 occasions in the Old Testament writings it was used to describe a change of relationship between man and God. This change of relationship involved a change of direction and a new beginning — a *conversion* (1979:289).

As Kasdorf views its theological usage, *shuv* "carries the idea of religious and ethical conversion in the sense of *turning* away from sin, *turning* to the Lord, *changing* one's course of direction, action, attitude, and relationship" (1980:42). As Price understands *shuv*, the term may be used in either of two valid senses:

> Negatively it may be *turning back* to iniquities and other gods (Jer 11:10); or *turning away* from the Lord himself (Num 14:43). Positively this conversion is *turning from* wickedness or transgression (Ezek 18:27ff); *turning towards God* (1979:289).

Old Testament Illustrations of Conversion

A more comprehensive understanding of conversion comes not only from a study of the Hebrew word *shuv* but also from illustrations of conversion in the Old Testament. The Mosaic period and the period of the kings and prophets provide examples which illustrate the meaning of conversion.

The Mosaic Period

"They have been quick to turn away from what I commanded them" (Exod 32:8). With this reproach God expressed His displeasure towards Israel for making a golden calf to worship while Moses was on Mount Sinai. But the worship of the golden calf was only a dramatic expression of a permanent drift away from God which Moses denounced later with stinging words of rebuke: "From the day you left Egypt until you arrived here, you have been rebellious against the LORD. . . . You have been rebellious against the LORD ever since I have known you" (Deut 9:7,24). Nevertheless, when Moses and the people confessed their sin and made a new commitment to God, He renewed His covenant with them (Exod 32–34).

Marc-Francois Lacan sees a similar pattern during the time of the judges. After Israel entered the promised land, their history developed as follows:

[There was] a succession of phases whose cycle is always the same: the people forsake Yahweh (Jg 2:12) and Yahweh delivers them over to their enemies (Jg 2:14); "the children of Israel cry to Yahweh and Yahweh raises up for them a savior" (Jg 3:9; cf. 3:15; 6:7; 10:10-16) (1978:80).

Price says it this way:

In the time of the judges it was the cry to God and the turning from sin that brought deliverance to the people of God (Judg 10:10,16; 1 Sam 7:3,4). Personalized inward repentance and turning was the reality from which the external acts of offerings, libations and fasting flowed (Judg 20:26) (1979:293).

The Period of the Kings and the Prophets

Sadly, Saul, the first king of Israel, illustrates a failure to turn back to the Lord. Saul's words of confession were good: "I have sinned. I violated the LORD's command and your instructions" (1 Sam 15:24). But his direction of life did not correspond with his words.

On the other hand, the fall and the return of King David present an Old Testament conversion that was authentic. David's sin was at least threefold: first, adultery with Bathsheba; second, the murder of her husband, Uriah; and third, giving occasion to the Ammonites to blaspheme the God of the Israelites (2 Sam 11 and 12). As long as David "kept silent," his "bones wasted away" through his "groaning all day long." He felt that the "hand" of God was "heavy" upon him (Ps 32:3-4). When Nathan, the prophet of God, rebuked his king, David said, "I have sinned against the LORD" (2 Sam 12:13). Unlike Saul, David's repentance and confession were complete and without rationalization. He confessed his sinful nature as well as his sinful acts, his sin against God as well as against his fellow man (Ps 51:1-5). For all time to come, both his sin and his return to the Lord became part of the Scriptures which would be read publicly. His prayer was humble and contrite:

> Create in me a pure heart, O God,
>   and renew a steadfast spirit within me.
> Do not cast me from your presence
>   or take your Holy Spirit from me.
> Restore to me the joy of your salvation
>   and grant me a willing spirit, to sustain me
>   (Ps 51:10-12).

David pictured his life direction changing so completely that, after his conversion, he would teach other transgressors God's ways and sinners would "turn back" to God (Ps 51:13). Lacan finds in David's conversion the "essential elements" of a true conversion:

> God initiates it; conversion is a grace. It is a grace of light which reveals to the sinner both his sin and the goodness of the one he has offended. The converted person receives the grace by humbly admitting his sin, and by opening himself with confidence to the goodness which wants to pardon him (1978:79).

Solomon, in his dedicatory prayer for the temple and for those who would worship there, stressed the need for God's sinful people to turn back (*shuv*) to Him with all their heart and soul (1 Kgs 8:46-48). The need for God's sinful people to return to Him was often stressed during this period. Yet, as Elijah saw so clearly, their conversion was a response to God's initiative. Because of this, during the great contest on Mount Carmel, he prayed, "Answer me, O LORD, answer me, so these people will know that you, O LORD, are God, and that you are turning their hearts back again" (1 Kgs 18:37). God was turning the hearts of those whose hearts needed to turn to God. The initiative was divine. The response was human.

The urgent call to repentance was heard throughout this period. Amos was astonished that, in spite of hunger, drought, poor harvests, plagues and violent overthrow, God's message was, "yet you have not returned (*shuv*) to me" (Amos 4:6,8-11). Ezekiel warned the exiles with God's clear call to conversion: "As surely as I live, declares the Sovereign LORD, I take no pleasure in the death of the wicked, but rather that they turn from their ways and live. Turn! Turn from your evil ways! Why will you die, O house of Israel?" (Ezek 33:11). Jeremiah was given a message in which the sins of the people of Judah were rebuked and in which he was to ask with a lament why they had not returned to the Lord:

> When men fall down, do they not get up?
>> When a man turns away, does he not return?
> Why then have these people turned away?
>> Why does Jerusalem always turn away?
> They cling to deceit;
>> they refuse to return.
> I have listened attentively,
>> but they do not say what is right.
> No one repents of his wickedness,
>> saying, "What have I done?"
> Each pursues his own course
>> like a horse charging into battle (Jer 8:4b-6).

According to Kasdorf, the root form of *shuv* occurs six times in the lament:

> Like the pair of verbs "fall" and "rise" (v.4b) describe opposites in a vertical direction, so the pair "turns" or "turn away" and "return" or "turn back" (v.4c) implies opposites in horizontal direction (1980:43).

Joel's call to repentance has an urgent ring of immediacy:

> "Even now," declares the LORD,
>> "return to me with all your heart,
>> with fasting and weeping and mourning."
>
> Rend your heart
>> and not your garments.
> Return to the LORD your God (Joel 2:12-13b).

In their passion for true inward repentance the prophets at times seem to call for a sweeping rejection of all outward rituals of repentance or worship. Isaiah pictures God as having "more than enough" of sacrifices, "detesting" incense, being "weary of bearing" and even "hating" their "New Moon festivals and [their] appointed feasts," and refusing to listen to the prayers of His people (Isa 1:10-15). Micah sees that "burnt offerings," "ten thousand rivers of oil," or even the sacrifice of his own child were not enough to "come before the LORD" (Micah 6:6-7). Amos stresses the same theme, saying that God "hated," "despised" and "could not stand" the "religious feasts" and the "assemblies" of His people, and that He would not "accept" their offerings (Amos 5:21-22). From this, one might conclude that God was totally rejecting the whole Pentateuch system of forms and rituals.

Instead, what the Lord rejected was strict observance of outward forms by those who were neglecting the inner realities of true repentance (Isa 1:15-19). The Lord rejected participation in outward forms of ritual repentance by the worshiper who neglected the proper internal meaning of the forms (Amos 5:22). The prophets called for the Lord's people to accompany the God-ordained forms with Godly living, with justice rolling on "like a river," and "righteousness like a never-failing stream" (Amos 5:24). They insisted that the people return to God whom they "had so greatly revolted against" (Isa 31:6). God's people should accompany their external rituals of repentance by turning away from the following:

- idolatrous worship (Hos 2:17; 13:1; Jer 1–4);
- foreign alliances (Isa 30:1-5,15);
- immorality and personal evil (Hos 4:1-3);
- empty nominal religious ritual (Hos 6:1-6; and
- social injustice and evil (Amos 4:1; 5:7-24)
  (Price 1979:296).

When this happened, when there was a true hunger and thirst for righteousness, when there was true inner repentance that issued in changed daily lives as well as outward ritual forms, then God would pardon his rebellious people. Isaiah summarizes the prophetic call to conversion with assurance of God's pardon in the following way:

> Seek the LORD while he may be found;
>   call on him while he is near.
> Let the wicked forsake his way
>   and the evil man his thoughts.
> Let him turn to the LORD, and he will have mercy on him,
>   and to our God, for he will freely pardon.
> "For my thoughts are not your thoughts,
>   neither are your ways my ways," declares the LORD.
> "As the heavens are higher than the earth,
>   so are my ways higher than your ways
>   and my thoughts than your thoughts" (Isa 55:6-9).

Yes. In general, God's ways are higher than ours — His thoughts are higher than ours. These are marvelous realities to remember as we face trials, crises and mysteries that transcend human understanding. But, in context, the *marvel is conversion.* We wicked, evil human beings can "forsake" our "ways" and "thoughts." We can "turn to the LORD" who will "have mercy" and "freely pardon" us. Why? *"For* my thoughts are not your thoughts, neither are your ways my ways," declares the Lord. God's ways and thoughts are so much higher than ours that He extends mercy and pardon to evil, wicked people who turn to Him, *to those who convert.*

Old Testament Theology of Conversion

These familiar, yet ever-new, words of Isaiah emphasize that conversion in the Old Testament was primarily a human response to the merciful God who was eager to pardon those who turned to him. God constantly taught Israel of His uniqueness and His holiness. Nevertheless, His people turned away from Him repeatedly to follow other gods. Israel went astray like an adulterous wife, but God would win her back if she would repent (Hos 1,2). In fact, His love was so great that He would even extend it beyond Israel to those called "Not my loved one." He would say to those called "Not my people," "You are my people," and they would say, "You are my God" (Hos 2:23). Thus, an Old Testament theology of conversion is rooted in the very nature of the unique, holy, yet loving, Lord whose thoughts and ways are so very much higher than human thoughts and ways!

It should, however, be remembered that most of those whom the prophets called to conversion were already in covenant relationship with God. By their sins, rebellions, and wicked ways they had turned away from God and their special relationship with Him. God's prophets were usually calling these covenant-breakers to convert by returning to Him. But, even then, God was also concerned with those who were not of the house of Israel. He used even the reluctant prophet Jonah to lead the Ninevites to repentance. "When God saw what they did and how they turned from their evil ways, he had compassion and did not bring upon them the destruction he had threatened" (Jonah 3:10).

Without doubt, God is concerned with the collective or national aspects of conversion, as Paul Löffler (1966:3-4) and Christopher Barth (1967:310) point out. Yet, national repentance is possible only as individuals repent. Jeremiah's repeated call was for individual, personal conversion: "So turn from your evil ways, each one of you, and reform your ways and your actions" (Jer 18:11; 25:5; 26:3; 36:3,7). Corporate, national conversion results from individual conversion so that, according to Walther Eichrodt, "In the re-creation of the individual, and nowhere else, God achieves the re-creating of his congregation" (1967:246). Hence, Old Testament conversion was corporate conversion by being basically individual, personal conversion.

What the person turned from in Old Testament conversion was sin. According to Kasdorf, "The root meaning of what we call 'sin' can be traced back to the Old Testament noun *chet*, sinfulness or being sinful, and the verb *chata*, to act sinfully" (1980:39). Although sin did appear as specific individual acts of idolatry, adultery, theft or murder, it also was seen as a state of rebellion against God (Isa 1:2) or of forsaking the Lord (Jer 1:16; 2:13,17,19). Therefore, as Price concluded, sin in the Old Testament was "a wrong attitude to Yahweh, a rebellion expressed in diverse acts of personal disobedience" (1979:302).

The convert, then, was one who turned from such acts and the rebellious attitude which produced them to trust in the Lord God and to submission to His holy will. Conversion was an inward change with respect to sin which led to outward changes in the convert's life, attitudes, and relationships.

Hence, Old Testament theology of conversion is rooted in the holy, yet loving, nature of God, the personal accountability and sinfulness of fallen humanity and the redemptive purposes of God in the salvation history of Israel. New Testament conversion concepts grow from this Old Testament rootage.

The New Testament Unfolding of Conversion Concepts

The Biblical concept of conversion which has such deep Old Testament rootage unfolds itself or comes to its fruitage in New Testament teaching and practice.

New Testament Language of Conversion

The conversion concepts included in the Hebrew word *shuv* are "taken up, expressed and developed in the New Testament by two word groups which deal with its various aspects. These are *epistrepho* and *metanoeo*" (Price 1979:308).

Epistrepho: to turn about, return, be converted

The word ἐπιστρέφω (*epistrepho*) does not have a meaning which is inherently sacred or religious. "In classical and secular Greek," according to Barclay, "it is a common word, and it has no technical religious sense at all" (1963:18). Like the word *shuv* which it "regularly translates . . . in the LXX" (Smalley 1964a:217) *epistrepho* is used quite often even in the New Testament to describe the mere physical act of turning or of returning. Thus an evil spirit said, "I will *return* to the house I left" (Matt 12:44), the shepherds *returned* to their fields near Bethlehem (Luke 2:20), Joseph and Mary *returned* to Galilee (Luke 2:39), Jesus "*turned* around in the crowd" to see who touched Him (Mark 5:30), Peter "*turned* and saw . . . the disciple whom Jesus loved" (John 21:20), or at the "end of the age" no one who is in the field is to "*go back* to get his cloak" (Matt 24:18), to mention some of the New Testament usages of *epistrepho* with its usual, literal meaning.

Epistrepho, therefore, was, like the Hebrew word *shuv*, an ordinary word which came to be used in a special religious or spiritual sense. This use of *epistrepho* to mean a spiritual turn or conversion is quite frequent in the New Testament. Barclay lists, among others, the following references of such special usage:

> "Repent," says Peter, "and turn again, that your sins may be blotted out" (Acts 3:19). When Peter healed Aeneas, all the residents of Lydda and Sharon saw him, and they turned to the Lord (Acts 9:35). During the preaching at Antioch a great number that believed turned to the Lord (Acts 11:21). It is Paul's appeal at Lystra that the people should turn from these vain things to a living God (Acts 14:15). It is the decision of the Jerusalem Council that the Gentiles who turn to God should not be troubled (Acts 15:19). It is Paul's conviction that he is divinely commissioned to open the eyes of the Gentiles that they may turn from darkness to light and from the power of Satan to God (Acts 26:18), and that they should repent and turn to God (1963:21-22).

In these references it is quite clear that *epistrepho* refers to what is normally meant by conversion. It means "a fundamentally new turning of the human will to God, a return home from blindness and error to the Saviour of all" (Fritz Laubach 1975: 355).

What is true of *epistrepho* is also true of its cognates, στρέφω (*strepho*) and ἐπιστροφή (*epistrophe*). These, too, are ordinary words which are used either to describe literal or spiritual turnings (Smalley 1964a:218). The spiritual use of the verb *strepho* is much less frequent than *epistrepho*; and the noun *epistrophe* is used only once in the New Testament, on the occasion when Paul and Barnabas, en route to the Jerusalem Council, visited Phoenicia and Samaria, "reporting the *conversion* of the Gentiles" (Acts 15:3, RSV).

Metanoeo: to change one's mind, repent, be converted

Again, as with *shuv* and *epistrepho*, the word μετανοέω (*metanoeo*) does not have a meaning which is basically or inherently sacred or religious. Barclay gives this explanation:

> The meaning of *metanoia* is clear; it means an *after-thought*. *Meta* is *afterwards* and *noia* is a *thought*. It is the exact opposite of *pronoia*, which means *forethought*, and the Greek moralists said that a wise man would always use *pronoia*, and then *metanoia* would be unnecessary. Originally and by derivation, *metanoia* simply meant the condition in which man had second thoughts about something (1963:48).

But the word *metanoeo* "is used with such force in the New Testament that it came to express far more than its etymology would suggest" (Gilliland 1983:104). Both John the Baptist and Jesus preached, "Repent, for the kingdom of heaven is near" (Matt 3:2; 4:17) and John preached "a baptism of repentance for the forgiveness of sins (Mark 1:4; Luke 3:3). When Jesus first sent out the Twelve, "they went out and preached that people should repent" (Mark 6:12). Those killed by Pilate or by the fall of the tower in Siloam were not "worse sinners" or "more guilty than all the others," Jesus warned, "But unless you repent, you too will all perish" (Luke 13:3,5). Jesus even taught that there is "rejoicing in heaven" over sinners who "repent" (Luke 15:7,10). Peter urged his hearers on Pentecost, "Repent and be baptized, every one of you, in the name of Jesus Christ for the forgiveness of your sins" (Acts 2:38) and soon thereafter preached, "Repent, then, and turn to God, so that your sins may be wiped out" (Acts 3:19). Paul told "the meeting of the Areopagus" that God "now . . . commands all people everywhere to repent" (Acts 17:30). Paul's message to "both Jews and Greeks" was that "they must turn to God in repentance and have faith in our Lord Jesus" (Acts 20:21). He told Agrippa that he preached "in Damascus," "in Jerusalem," "in all Judea" and "to the Gentiles also" that "they should repent and turn to God and prove their repentance by their deeds" (Acts 26:20). Thus, as Gilliland observed, "Beginning with Peter's Pentecost sermon, no apostolic preaching was complete without the uncompromising call to repentance" (1983:104).

What a person was called to in repentance was more than a new judgment on some previous action or regret for the consequences of such an action. Instead, "Repentance is the awakened awareness of past sin . . . a genuine sorrow for the wrong thing; a genuine shame for the feelings and the motives which inspired it; a genuine discovery that the thing was wrong in the sight of God" (Barclay 1963:48-49).

Repentance was not a mere sense of remorse. Rather, it was a change of heart and mind with reference to sin, produced by Godly sorrow which "brings repentance that leads to salvation and leaves no regret" (2 Cor 7:10). The concept of repentance in the New Testament takes us far beyond a mere intellectual activity to a change which involves "the personality of the individual as a whole" (Smalley 1964a:224). Hence, we may summarize with Price: "Both *epistrepho* and *metanoeo* complement one another in pointing to the New Testament meaning of conversion. The different emphases they bring should be held in tension and 'flesh out' our understanding of what it means for a man to be converted" (1979:312-313).

New Testament Illustrations of Conversion

Beginning with this linguistic information, we can also "flesh out" our understanding of conversion by looking at illustrations of conversion in the New Testament. Cases of conversion recorded in Acts are important for this study, but these are best seen against the background of the preaching of repentance and conversion by John the Baptist, Jesus, and the early church.

John the Baptist: Preaching Repentance

After the voice of prophecy had not been heard for centuries in Israel, "The word of God came to John son of Zechariah in the desert. He went into all the country around the Jordan, preaching a baptism of repentance for the forgiveness of sins" (Luke 3:2-3). Thus, John fulfilled not only the prophecy concerning "a voice of one calling in the desert" to "prepare the way for the Lord" (Luke 3:4) but also the angel's word to Zechariah concerning John: "Many of the people of Israel will he bring back to the Lord their God" (Luke 1:16). His conversion message, "Repent, for the kingdom of heaven is near" (Matt 3:1) was for all the people, including even the religious establishment who thought they had no need to repent (Matt 3:7-10). John stressed that repentance toward God would result in a new relationship with one's neighbors characterized by deeds or actions which were fruits of repentance (Luke 3:10-14). According to Price, " the message of John was clear, God has turned to men. Men need to *turn to Him* as they prepare for His coming" (1979:314). John announced "that God was about to take action, to manifest his kingly power; that in anticipation of this great event men must repent;

and as evidence of repentance must submit to baptism" (Ladd 1974:36). John's prophetic conversion message rejected all nationalistic views. According to Ladd, even Gentiles were to be included:

> The approach of God's Kingdom means that Jews can find no security in the fact that they were sons of Abraham; that Jews, apart from repentance, had no more certainty of entering the coming Kingdom than did Gentiles; that both Jews and Gentiles must repent and manifest that repentance by submitting to baptism (1974:41).

John's wilderness message not only renewed the urgent Old Testament prophetic call to repentance, but it also transcended Judaism and pointed toward Him whose sandals John was "not worthy to untie" (Luke 3:16).

Jesus Christ: Preaching the Kingdom

The voice of John had attracted the attention of Israel. Now, He who is "more powerful" than John, He whose sandals John is not "worthy to stoop down and untie" (Mark 1:7), has come. What was His message? According to Mark, "After John was put in prison, Jesus went into Galilee, proclaiming the good news of God. 'The time has come,' he said. 'The kingdom of God is near. Repent and believe the good news'!" (Mark 1:14-15).

There is a broad consensus among Biblical scholars that the Kingdom of God was the central message of Jesus (Ladd 1974: 57). Jesus constantly proclaimed the Kingdom: throughout Galilee (Matt 4:23; 9:35); when He taught His disciples in parables (Matt 13:10-52); when little children were brought to Him (Mark 10:13-16); in His conversation with Nicodemus (John 3:1-10); when responding to the faith of a Roman centurion (Matt 8:5-13); and even during His trial before Pilate (John 18:33-37). He taught His disciples to pray, "your kingdom come, your will be done on earth as it is in heaven" (Matt

6:10). Jesus taught, "And this gospel of the kingdom will be preached in the whole world as a testimony to all nations, and then the end will come" (Matt 24:14).

What did Jesus preach when He proclaimed "the Kingdom of God"? The phrase, "the Kingdom of God," has an inherent complexity which not only defies precise definition but also allows multiple meanings to be attached to it. However, the main thrust of the term "Kingdom of God" is the rule or the reign of God in the hearts and lives of those who submit to His Sovereign Will. According to Donald Kraybill, "Biblical scholars generally agree that the term 'kingdom of God' indicates the dynamic rule or reign of God. The kingdom of God occurs when persons are ruled by God" (1978:25). Ladd asserts: "The Kingdom of God is His kingship, His rule, His authority" and that, when we "seek first his kingdom" we are seeking "His sway, His rule, His reign in our lives. . . . The Kingdom of God is basically the rule of God. It is God's reign, the divine sovereignty in action" (1959:21,24). Arthur Glasser views the Kingdom of God as "one of the central, overarching themes of the Bible" and understands Jesus' use of these important words to mean "the saving and ruling presence of God over His people" (1983: 32,37). Hence, when Jesus preached the Kingdom of God, He preached the Reign of God in the lives of His people.

There is, moreover, a link in the preaching of Jesus between the Reign or Kingdom of God and human conversion. "The kingdom of God is near. Repent and believe the good news" (Mark 1:15). As we have seen, repentance is more than remorse or regret for the consequences of past actions. Instead, it is "the awakened awareness of past sin. . . . a genuine sorrow for the wrong thing . . . a genuine discovery that the thing was wrong in the sight of God" (Barclay 1963:48-49). But to produce repentance God must intervene. He must encounter the sinner who is in need of conversion. This He does through the message of the Kingdom. Whoever hears the message hears good news which is capable of turning the sinner around or causing repentance if the message is believed.

The preaching of Jesus called sinful humanity to enter the Kingdom through conversion, as Werner Kümmel points out:

> If this call to repentance is directed to all men, it must be presumed that all men need such a conversion; and from that it can be concluded that the prevalence of sin in all men is, for Jesus, a self-evident element in His view of man, even if it is not dogmatically formulated (1963:19).

Since all humanity is sinful, Jesus calls all humanity to a radical conversion by His Kingdom message. Sinners are to be "born again" in order to "see" or to "enter" the Kingdom of God (John 3:3-5). Only those who "change and become like little children" can enter the Kingdom (Matt 18:3).

Those who heard the Kingdom message of Jesus responded in different ways. Some rejected Him and His message (John 1:10-11). He was called a blasphemer (Mark 2:7), a charge on which He was finally condemned to die (Mark 14:63-64). Wealth hindered some (Mark 5:15-17; 10:21-25), and others rejected Him because of religious self-satisfaction (Matt 5:20; Luke 18:9-14) and hypocrisy (Matt 23:5,13,15,25). The sin of attributing to the prince of demons the miracle-working power of the Holy Spirit in Jesus was an obstacle so serious as to render conversion impossible (Mark 3:22-30).

But others followed Him. Among them were Peter, Andrew, and the sons of Zebedee who left their occupations to follow Him (Mark 1:16-20). Later Levi, the publican, followed Him (Mark 2:14). Not only the woman at the well but also "many of the Samaritans from that town believed in him" because of her testimony (John 4:39). Although some of the crowd who came to the Jewish Feast of Tabernacles called Him "demon-possessed" and tried to seize Him, others said, "surely this man is the Prophet" or "he is the Christ" (John 7:20,30,40-41).

John presents the responses to Jesus and His message as basically rejection or reception responses: "He came to that which was his own, but his own did not receive him. Yet to all who received him, to those who believed in his name, he gave the right to become children of God" (John 1:11-12).

Although Jesus would not allow the excited crowds who followed Him to make Him a military-political king (John 6:15) and assured Pilate that His Kingdom was "not of this world" (John 18:36), He, nevertheless, boldly told Caesar's representative, "You are right in saying I am a king" (John 18:37). His Kingdom was different, however, not only because His subjects "would [not] fight" (John 18:36) but most significantly because He was a king who would go to His crown by the way of a cross. As He was dying, some jeered at "this King of Israel" (Mark 15:32) and Pilate offended the "chief priests of the Jews" by having "a notice prepared and fastened to the cross. It read, JESUS OF NAZARETH, THE KING OF THE JEWS" (John 19:19,21). Both the priests and Pilate spoke greater truth than they knew. Jesus was, indeed, a king; but the Kingdom over which Jesus would rule could not be entered by a sword or a vote, but by conversion.

The Early Church: Preaching Christ Crucified-Resurrected

During a postresurrection appearance just prior to His being "taken up into heaven" (Luke 24:51), Jesus commissioned His disciples to preach "repentance and forgiveness of sins . . . in his name to all nations, beginning at Jerusalem" (Luke 24:47). This mandate, based on His death and resurrection, continued the call for conversion and pointed toward its wider dimensions among the nations or the ἔθνη (*ethne*).

The early church executed this commission by preaching which led to conversion. Although scholars differ on the precise points included in the ancient κήρυγμα (*kerygma*), I concur with Smalley who wrote of this as follows:

> The central point of the apostolic *kerygma* is the redemptive activity of God in Christ. The incarnation, death, and resurrection of Jesus Christ, which are the basic elements of the preaching, manifestly appear as acts of God. Through and

through, the work of salvation is His. It is God who attests
the man, and glorifies His servant, Jesus (Acts 2:22; 3:13);
it is He who raises from the dead the Author of life, killed
with His own foreknowledge (Acts 3:15; 2:23; 10:40ff.). In
other words, the apostles recount the *heilsgeschichte* which
has become centered in God's final visitation (1964a:221).

Paul summarized the apostolic message which the Corinthians
had "received" and by which they were "saved" in these words:

> Now, brothers, I want to remind you of the gospel I
> preached to you, which you received and on which you
> have taken your stand. By this gospel you are saved, if you
> hold firmly to the word I preached to you. Otherwise, you
> have believed in vain. For what I received I passed on to
> you as of first importance: that Christ died for our sins
> according to the Scriptures, that he was buried, that he was
> raised on the third day according to the Scriptures (1 Cor
> 15:1-4).

The early church preached this basic message and called for the
conversion of those who heard it.

Cases of Conversion in Acts

Both Price (1979:321-336) and Smalley (1964a:222-224)
examine in considerable detail the following cases of individual
conversion which Luke records in Acts: the Ethiopian eunuch
(8:26-40); Paul (9:1-31; 22:1-16; 26:1-23); Cornelius (10:1-
48; 11:1-18); Lydia (16:11-15) and the Philippian jailer
(16:16-34).

Smalley sees a "fairly consistent pattern — discernible in
each case of conversion" (1964a:222) and Price agrees that,
although the converts are of "different backgrounds, nationali-
ty, sex and personality," and although the conversions occur "in
very different circumstances," nevertheless, "there are features
that are common between them" (1979:321).

In passing, Smalley notes the "impressive fact that in no case
does anything like an explicit confession of faith occur by itself,

and apart from baptism" (1964a:222). He then itemizes the six stages of conversion as follows: (1) preparation; (2) preaching about Jesus or His presence; (3) inquiry; (4) the activity of God; (5) baptism; and (6) results (1964a:222-223). After discussing these stages in more detail, Smalley again stresses the place of baptism by noting that in these cases of conversion "only one stage belongs inseparably to them all; and that is the baptism of the convert" (1964a:223).

Price adopts Smalley's "stages," adds two to the list, and calls them "factors" which he then lists as follows:

1. The period of preparation;
2. The proclamation of the word by a witness;
3. The perception of the hearer;
4. The point of encounter;
5. The personal confession of the convert in baptism;
6. The participation in a Christian community;
7. The practical results of conversion; and
8. The power of the Spirit of God throughout the process (1979:323).

Price acknowledges that this is a "western cultural approach to the analysis of the conversions in Acts" and suggests that "it be kept in mind that they merge together to form the organic whole of the experience of conversion" (1979:323).

After intensive study of cases of individual conversion in Acts within the framework of these eight factors, Price reached the following conclusions:

> *First*, there is great variation in the actual details of the conversion process in each case. There is no one fixed conversion experience that all must have or imitate, except that baptism is common to all.
> *Second*, the common constant of conversion for each person was their turning to God through commitment to Jesus Christ. . . .
> *Third*, conversion is part of the total biography of life. . . .
> *Fourth*, conversion takes place in response to a preaching or sharing of the good news. . . .

Fifth, the mind of the convert is active in understanding the good news and its implications for behavior. . . . there is a respect for the whole personality and the free will of man.

Sixth, there is a sense in which we may speak of a point of encounter in conversion which is individual and personal, . . .

Seventh, baptism is closely related with conversion but is not identical with it. . . .

Eighth, conversion is personal, individual, but not private as it relates to participation and involvement in the Body of Christ. . . .

Ninth, conversion is a vertical response to God which issues in radical changes in daily life and relationships with our fellow man. . . .

Tenth, the Holy Spirit is the author of conversion, for it is the work of God. . . . The reception of the Holy Spirit is linked in Acts with conversion. . . . In this sense Christian conversion may be said to be unique to all other forms of conversion as it alone brings man into a personal relationship with the living God (1979:334-336).

While Smalley recognizes the "limitations of our evidence," he does think there are enough features "common to all these accounts for certain general deductions to be permitted." They are as follows:

First, the spiritual experience in question is more than simply the work of a moment; second, it is frequently occasioned by preaching; third, some kind of intellectual activity, however elementary, is involved; fourth, the conversion is undertaken by an individual who is treated as a whole personality; fifth, the believer is related more or less immediately to the total life of the Church by the instrument of baptism, often directly associated with the gift of the Spirit; and finally, as the premise of all that may be said about conversion in the New Testament, the work is from first to last a response to the *opus Dei* [work of God] (1964a:223-224).

Similar deductions can also be drawn from the multi-individual or multipersonal cases of conversion in Acts. After Peter's sermon on Pentecost, "Those who accepted his message were baptized, and about three thousand were added to their number that day" (Acts 2:41). In Samaria "when they believed Philip as he preached the good news of the kingdom of God and the name of Jesus Christ, they were baptized, both men and women" (Acts 8:12).

New Testament Theology of Conversion

In the New Testament, conversion was primarily a human response to the gracious God who was eager to pardon those of all nations who turned to Him through commitment to Jesus Christ. In Christ, God the Father has uniquely revealed Himself to fallen humanity (John 14:6-9), and He has acted savingly for us through the cross. "God was reconciling the world to himself in Christ" (2 Cor 5:19). Christ crucified was the "power of God and the wisdom of God" for both Jews and Greeks who did not previously know Him (1 Cor 1:21-25).

The power was not in animal sacrifices, the latest intellectual fashion or in mere human righteousness but in Christ Jesus whom "God presented . . . as a sacrifice of atonement, through faith in his blood" (Rom 3:25). The gospel of Christ crucified, buried and resurrected (1 Cor 15:1-4) was the "power of God for the salvation of everyone who believes: first for the Jew, then for the Gentile" (Rom 1:16,17). No one could come to God except through Christ (John 14:6) who came to save a perishing world (John 3:16).

The Holy Spirit whom Jesus promised His disciples as a "Counselor" (John 14:15) came on them on Pentecost and "filled" them and "enabled" them as they proclaimed the gospel (Acts 2). The Holy Spirit was also involved in case after case of the conversion accounts in Acts.

God as Father, Son and Spirit took the initiative in the "turning" of sinful humanity from their "wicked ways" (Acts 3:26). Hence, the basis for a New Testament theology of conversion is rooted in the very nature of the unique, holy, yet

loving God who does not want "anyone to perish, but everyone to come to repentance" (2 Pet 3:9).

What sinners were called to in New Testament conversion
was a radical change produced by belief in the message of a
Kingdom whose King went to His crown by the way of a crucifixion. Fallen humanity, whether Jewish or Greek, was urged to
"turn to God in repentance and have faith in our Lord Jesus"
(Acts 20:21). In view of the utterly amazing truth that "God
has made this Jesus, whom you crucified, both Lord and
Christ" (Acts 2:36), sinners were commanded: "Repent and be
baptized, every one of you, in the name of Jesus Christ for the
forgiveness of your sins. And you will receive the gift of the
Holy Spirit" (Acts 2:38).

Whether expressed in terms of guilt or shame, those who
were "separate from Christ" were "without hope and without
God in the world" (Eph 2:12). The change produced by conversion was so radical that converts were "no longer foreigners
and aliens, but fellow citizens with God's people and members
of God's household" (Eph 2:19). Converts in the New
Testament were called out of a past in which they were "dead
in . . . transgressions and sins" (Eph 2:1) and into a new life in
Christ and in His body, the church (Eph 1:22-23; Col 1:18).

As we have seen from our survey of Acts, New Testament
conversion was a process which involved: a period of preparation in the life of the convert; the proclamation of the gospel;
perception and faith on the part of the hearer; a point of encounter in which sinners are called to repent; baptism; incorporation into the church; changed lives and the power of the
Holy Spirit. Even though the point of encounter may be fairly
sudden or dramatic as in Paul's case (Acts 9,16,22), there was,
nevertheless, a more gradual period of preparation which was
part of the whole process of conversion (Gilliland 1983:77-80).

Although God was always the prime mover in conversion,
sinners are viewed as responsible beings who could receive or
reject the conversion message even when it was presented by
Christ Himself or one of His apostles.

A study of New Testament teaching on the topic leads me to concur with Gilliland that conversion is "at once the most important, the most personal, and the most spiritual phenomenon of mission" (1983:71). A comprehensive view of conversion in the New Testament leads also to Gilliland's conclusion:

> Conversion is normative for mission. It is the self-evident, a priori event, however experienced or understood, that both initiates and afterward nurtures the Christian life. In simplest terms, the non-Christian cannot be a Christian without *becoming* a Christian. Conversion is *becoming* a Christian. Conversion is entering into the new life. There is no way to describe mission to the non-Christian world without being very candid about this greatest of miracles (1983:72).

New Testament theology of conversion, therefore, is rooted in the nature of God who has expressed His Fatherly care through the Incarnate Son who dies and ever lives for sinners and through the Spirit who confronts sinners and enables converts to live the new life of love in the church. Although alienated from God by the shame and guilt of sin, fallen humanity is capable of responding as penitent believers to God's conversion call. This repentant faith is expressed in baptism when the convert completes the initial conversion process and enters the church to share its fellowship, teaching, love and mission.

Chapter III

BAPTISM

Having surveyed the Biblical meaning of conversion, we shall now turn to a general background study of baptism. A study of "Antecedents of Christian Baptism," "Baptism as Ritual Symbolism," and "Baptism as Sacrament" will widen our frame of reference for further study of the role of baptism in Pauline theology of conversion. To place our background study in as wide a context as is needed we shall turn first to study the antecedents of Christian baptism.

Antecedents of Christian Baptism

Christian baptism did not begin in a vacuum. Instead, it originated among the Jews, a people already familiar with the use of water for various lustrations (Lev 12–15). It arose within a society which used immersion as an act of ritual cleansing (W.O.E. Oesterley and G.H. Box 1907:256).

Moreover, as Edward P. Myers points out, "the practice of ritual lustrations, as practiced by the Jewish people in the religion of Israel has a long history behind it" (1986:1). In fact, "from very early times water has been used . . . for the purpose of religious lustration. The practice is common in all parts of the world and at all stages of the history of religion" (W.F.

Flemington 1948:ix). Hence, the most remote ancestry of Christian baptism can be traced back even beyond the religion of Israel to ancient non-Jewish lustrations.

Ancient Non-Jewish Lustrations

That Christian baptism can be traced back through Judaism to ancient non-Jewish ritual cleansings should not surprise the careful student, for similarity between such practices implies only similarity, not necessarily a borrowing or a dependence. Beasley-Murray reminds us that we could "draw a direct line of development from the witch doctor and his practices to the modern medical practitioner and his methods, but we do not normally confound the latter with the former" (1962:2). Even though we may recognize a link between current beliefs, practices, or customs and those of remote times and even acknowledge an indebtedness to prior cultures for what we now have, we do not usually confuse origins with later developments. And, as Beasley-Murray points out,

> The Old Testament lustrations are linked with sacrificial worship; but no one is under the illusion that sacrifices to Deity were first observed among the Jews, nor are people generally surprised to learn that the ordinances as to their performance and significance are not unrelated to sacrificial thought and practice that go back to remote times among many peoples. So also ritual cleansings in water were practiced from immemorial antiquity (1962:1).

According to Myers, "lustration rites have been practiced by nearly all primitive people" (1986:2). J.A. MacCulloch discusses various water rites used by such ancient non-Jewish peoples as African, American and Polynesian tribal groups (1928:2:367-375). Whether these rituals were simple or complex, water in such ceremonies was seen as a means of cleansing. It was thought by those who attributed magical powers to water that just as water cleansed dirt from the physical body it could also "cleanse spiritual pollution as well" (Myers 1986:2).

Markus Barth depicted early belief in the power found in water as follows:

> By the grace of the deity involved, through the knowledge and administration of the ministrant, and according to the faith of those initiated, the water rites bring into effect what they symbolize, and they demonstrate what they effect (1969:85).

Mircea Eliade wrote of the ancient belief that water possessed qualities which would bring new life. Water was seen as the "seed of things," "the origin of human life," "the universal mother," "the supreme magic and medicinal substance," and as the element which possesses the power of "purifying, of regenerating, of giving new birth; for what is immersed in it 'dies' and, rising again from the water, is like a child without any sin or any past, able to receive a new revelation and begin a new and *real* life" (1958:188-194). Eliade adds that the "immemorial and oecumenial [sic] symbolism of immersion in water as an instrument of purification and regeneration was adopted by Christianity and given still richer religious meaning" (1958:196).

Hence, Christian baptism began in a world already familiar with ritual ablutions and even ceremonial immersions long before the beginning of Jewish lustration rites. As Oscar Cullmann correctly pointed out, "Baptism as an external act is thus not the creation of Jesus" (1950:9). It is also correct to point out that baptism as an external act is not even the creation of the Jews.

Lustrations in the Old Testament

Nevertheless, the Old Testament contains many passages which present the practice of ritual washings for purification and cleansing. These passages make it clear that the Jews made frequent use of water for various lustrations.

According to the Old Testament, "uncleanness" could be the result of a number of different situations or actions, such as: (1) eating or touching unclean food (Lev 11); (2) childbirth (Lev 12:1-5); (3) infectious skin diseases (Lev 13:1-46); (4) mildew in clothing (Lev 13:47-59); (5) male bodily discharges (Lev 15:1-18); (6) female bodily discharges (Lev 15:19-32) and (7) touching a dead body (Num 19:11-22). Although there were similar laws and taboos among ancient non-Jewish ethnic groups,[1] Charles B. Williams thinks that this does not diminish our respect for the Old Testament laws on uncleanness:

> Might not Jeh [Yahweh] use this natural religious perception of men as to an intrinsic distinction between clean and unclean in training Israel to a realization of a higher conception — the real difference between sin and holiness, i.e. between moral defilement and moral purification? (1952: 3036).

Thus, by starting on a lower level, God trains His people to be holy as He is holy (Lev 11:44-45).

But how were the Jews to obtain purification from such uncleanness? The Old Testament presented various agencies and rituals for such purification. Myers points out that there were

> prescriptions for cleansing from (1) eating carcasses, Lev. 11:40; (2) touching, or being touched by, leprosy, Lev. 14:8ff; (3) sick discharges, Lev. 15:5ff, Deut. 23:12; (4) menstruation, Lev. 15:21f; (5) hemorrhage, Lev. 15:25ff; or (6) touching the dead, Numbers 19 (1986:5-6).

Although a study of cleansing by blood is beyond the scope of this book, the prominent place of blood sacrifices among the Jews is well known to students of the Old Testament. Blood was also used for purification or for ceremonial cleansing (Lev 14:5-7; 51:52; Num 19:4) with the provision that the blood was taken from a clean animal. Hence, water was not the only agency involved in Jewish rites of purification. It did, however, occupy an important place in them as Philip Wendell Crannell makes clear. Crannell maintains that, "For the elaborate system of ceremonial cleansing" recorded in the Old Testament, the

> principal agencies were water, alone, as in minor or indirect defilements, like those produced by contact with the unclean (Lev **15** 5-18, etc); or combined with a sin offering and burnt offering, as with a woman after childbirth (**12** 6-8); fire, as with gentile booty (Nu **31** 23; by water, when it would not endure the fire); the ashes of a red heifer without spot, mingled with running water, for those defiled by contact with the dead (Nu **19** 2ff). For the complex ceremonial in cases of leprosy, combining water, cedar, hyssop, crimson thread, the blood and flight of birds, the trespass offering, sin offering, burnt offering, see Lev **14** (1952:668).

Hence, ceremonial washings in water figured prominently in Old Testament rites of purification.

This emphasis on ceremonial purity must not be disparaged as mere "ritualism." Of course, God Himself desired an inner cleansing that would accompany ritual purity. God wanted inner purity, life purity, heart purity. Moreover, many of the Jews knew that true worship required more than external ablutions and purity. Pilgrims should approach temple worship in the following spirit:

> Who may ascend the hill of the LORD?
>   Who may stand in his holy place?
> He who has clean hands and a pure heart,
>   who does not lift up his soul to an idol
>   or swear by what is false (Ps 24:3-4).

Or, the penitent sinner would cry out,

> Have mercy on me, O God, . . .
> Wash away all my iniquity
>   and cleanse me from my sin. . . .
> Surely you desire truth in the inner parts; . . .
> Cleanse me with hyssop, and I will be clean;
>   wash me, and I will be whiter than snow. . . .

Create in me a pure heart, O God,
and renew a steadfast spirit within me (Ps 51:1ff).

But, although inner cleansing was stressed, Ezekiel, the prophet-priest, "conjoins spiritual cleansing with ceremonial purity" (Beasley-Murray 1962:9) when he depicts the Sovereign Lord as saying, "I will sprinkle clean water on you, and you will be clean; I will cleanse you from all your impurities and from all your idols" (Ezek 36:25). Moreover, although Jesus stressed purity of heart (Matt 5:8), He did not abolish Jewish lustration rites. Instead, He submitted to John's baptism (Matt 3:13-17) and rebuked the Pharisees for not doing so themselves (Mark 11:27-33). Therefore, Jewish lustration rites may be seen as foreshadowing Christian baptism. They were antecedents of it, at least in the sense that they were prior to it in time. Jews of Jesus' day were accustomed to the use of water for ritual purification.

Yet, in another sense, these Jewish lustrations are not the truest antecedents of Christian baptism since they were *repeated cleansings* and Christian baptism is a *once-for-all-rite.*

Flemington expresses this idea clearly:

> Such an intensified use of religious washings shows how entirely natural it was for a Jew to make use of water for purificatory purposes. It is not in these rites, however, that the antecedents of Christian baptism are to be sought. These ceremonies of lustration were not confined to one particular moment of a man's life; on the contrary, they were repeated as often as the need for purification might arise. An antecedent for Christian baptism may more appropriately be sought in some act of lustration performed once and for all, and moreover, an act associated with the transition from one state of life to another. Such an act was the Jewish rite known as "proselyte baptism" (1948:4).

Jewish Proselyte Baptism

So many scholars favor a pre-Christian date for the origin of Jewish proselyte baptism that Beasley-Murray could say that the "majority of investigators" regarded it as "axiomatic" (1962:18). Myers cites an impressive list of scholars as having written in favor of an "older origin" of proselyte baptism.[2] But why do the "majority of investigators" opt for a pre-Christian date for the origin of Jewish proselyte baptism?

According to H. Mueller, the rite of proselyte baptism must have been practiced by the Jews prior to Christian baptism because it was not likely that the Jews would have adopted it from a religious group toward which they were so antagonistic (1967:55). R.E.O. White agrees with this and says, "It appears extremely unlikely that a hostile Judaism would borrow any significant rite from the 'heretical sect of Christianity' (Acts xxiv 5) at any time between A.D. 35 and 95 when proselyte baptism was certainly practiced" (1960:320).

Flemington also agrees with the majority opinion when he stresses the "extreme improbability" of the view that Christian baptism was antecedent to the Jewish practice of the rite as follows:

> The use by New Testament writers of βαπτίσμα [*baptisma*] and its cognates of John's baptism, without any attempt to explain their meaning, is most intelligible if some similar rite were already in widespread use. Again, in view of the intense bitterness which existed between Judaism and the early Church, it would seem in the highest degree unlikely that the Jews would have borrowed so distinctive a practice from a Christian source (1948:4).

According to Beasley-Murray, Emil Schürer thought one consideration was enough to scatter all arguments against the early origin of proselyte baptism: "A Gentile, who did not observe the Levitical regulations concerning purity, was unclean as a matter of course, and so could not be admitted into Jewish communions without a tebilah, a ritual bath of purification" (1962:20). As Schürer himself expressed it, "This general consideration is of itself so conclusive that there is no need to lay any very great stress on individual testimonies" (1979:322).

Another impressive line of evidence in favor of a pre-Christian date for Jewish proselyte baptism arises out of the discussions of baptism which occurred when "Jews of Jerusalem" sent priests and Levites to John the Baptist to "ask him who he was" (John 1:19). When one reads John 1:19f, Mark 11:30 and parallels, it is interesting to note that

> the Sanhedrin's enquiry concerning John's baptism centered not upon its form or meaning, but only upon John's authority to perform it. The practice itself appears to be accepted as familiar. Had the rite been an innovation, we would expect their question to be "Why baptize . . .?"; precisely because they were themselves already practicing a baptism after the mode described, but with duly appointed witnesses, and with legal implications, they saw John's as an irregular, lay, unauthorised rite, and their question is: "Why baptisest *thou?*" (White 1960:320-321).

Seen in this light, it was not John's baptism which was an anomaly. The Sanhedrin were already familiar with that form and its meaning. What excited them was that John was baptizing without the authority of the religious establishment of Jerusalem. It was happening without the authority of the local *illuminati.*

Against the view that Jewish proselyte baptism predated Christian baptism is the fact that there is no mention of it in the Old Testament, the New Testament, Philo or Josephus, and no clear testimony to it in pre-Christian writings. But no one thinks the practice was old enough to be mentioned in the Old Testament. And as White points out,

> The silence of the New Testament is hardly strange, especially if the practice were so familiar as to require no explanation. Schürer contended that no one has shown where in Philo or Josephus any mention of the rite would have been expected; and Marsh thinks that familiarity would again make any direct reference unnecessary. Foakes-Jackson says that Philo and Josephus rarely mention the synagogue (1960:321).

Therefore, although it is difficult to establish the exact time of the origin of Jewish proselyte baptism, it is probable that, just as Jewish proselyting of Gentiles predated Christianity (Matt 23:15), so did Jewish proselyte baptism. Christian baptism did not begin until the A.D. 30s, because Christianity itself had its beginning then. But both the Jewish religion and its attempts to win converts from the Gentiles were practiced much earlier than Christianity. So also, it appears, was Jewish proselyte baptism.

According to Alex Gilmore the nature and significance of Jewish proselyte baptism can be summarized under five headings: (1) It was for convinced and instructed converts, and it was a witnessed ceremony. (2) It was an initiation ceremony, making a break with the old life, and a joyful acceptance of the new. (3) It was an act of dedication. (4) It carried with it the idea of cleansing. (5) It was more than a symbol or declaration; it was an effective sign (1959:68-70).

According to Flemington,

> proselyte baptism is essentially a rite of initiation into the new religion. By it a man signified that he abandoned the old life and entered into a new one. . . . Proselyte baptism was a ceremonial purification whereby a Gentile was enabled to enter the congregation of Israel. Since it was demanded by Jews, it must have been regarded as exercising an effect on the whole personality of the man submitting to it. . . . the fact that proselyte baptism was set in the context of the commandments meant that the way was always open for a more explicitly ethical interpretation of the rite. Such an adaptation and extension of the rite of proselyte baptism seems to have been first made by a Jewish prophet, who, towards the end of the second decade of the first century A.D., aroused notice by preaching on the banks of the River Jordan and by associating prominently with his message an act of baptism (1948:7,11).

Accordingly, we shall consider the "more explicitly ethical interpretation of the rite" as seen in the prophetic ministry of

John the Baptist. But first, let us take a look at the Qumran Community and their baptisms.

Baptism and the Qumran Community

The discovery of the Dead Sea Scrolls in 1947 at Khirbet Qumran has provided much information about a religious community that lived in an area near the Dead Sea. The community, made up of Jews who volunteered to separate themselves from mainstream Judaism which had been corrupted by worldliness and Hellenization, was established during the second century B.C. (Gilmore 1959:68-70). Usually called "Essenes," this group "numbered about four thousand and devoted themselves to a simplistic, disciplined lifestyle. They were basically monastic, practiced asceticism, and considered themselves the Israel within Israel" (Myers 1986:24).

According to Myers,

> There seemed to have been three distinct lustration practices at Qumran: (1) The daily ceremonial washings which were practiced early in the morning upon arising and were repeated before each meal. This ceremony was also practiced at other times. . . . (2) Annual lustrations which were performed annually, probably around Pentecost. (3) The initiation lustrations which were practiced at the time one became a part of the community . . . (1986:24-25).

But one must not suppose that the Qumran community sought for moral purity in lustration rites alone. As Beasley-Murray points out, they had "a clear understanding of the limitations of lustrations" as expressed in Chapters II and III of their Manual of Discipline. The manual affirms that the man who continues to walk in the stubbornness of his heart will not be admitted into the community since

> he cannot be cleared by mere ceremonies of atonement, nor cleansed by any waters of ablution, nor sanctified by immersion in lakes or rivers, nor purified by any bath. Unclean,

unclean he remains so long as he rejects the government of God and refuses the discipline of communion with Him. For it is only through the spiritual apprehension of God's truth that man's ways can be properly directed. Only thus can all his iniquities be shriven so that he can gaze upon the true light of life. . . . Only by a spirit of uprightness and humility can his sin be atoned. Only by the submission of his soul to all the ordinances of God can his flesh be made clean. Only thus can it really be sprinkled with waters of ablution (1962:13-14).

Hence, the outward cleansing alone was not adequate to bring purification. Outward cleansing had to be accompanied by inner purity. Purifying the flesh without repentance was of no value. But when there was true humility and submission, then the waters of ablution cleansed from sin and the waters of purification sanctified. As Beasley-Murray sees it, "it looks as though the first ablution of a novice was more than simply a first bath: it signified an entrance on to the state of purity and consequently an entrance into the company of the purified" (1962:17).

It is quite likely that the baptisms of the Qumran community were antecedents of John's baptism. Some even think John may have been an Essene who lived for a while at Qumran. At any rate, Beasley-Murray thinks there is a "bridge from Qumran to John the Baptist," a bridge which has "more than one track":

For the Covenanters and for John, the End is near; it requires drastic moral preparation; and lustration apart from the Temple worship, albeit necessarily conjoined with repentance, is effective for that purpose. In each case John is more radical in his teaching and more genuinely prophetic; but the Covenanters prepared the Way of the Lord better than they knew — by preparing the way of the Forerunner (1962:18).

The Baptism of John

When we think of that "Forerunner," John, the son of Zechariah, the priest, and Elizabeth, his previously barren wife, we immediately think of baptism. In fact, baptism was so important in John's prophetic mission that he was called the "baptizer" or the "baptist" (Matt 3:1; Mark 6:14).

Mark dates the beginning of the gospel about Jesus Christ from the time when John the baptizer fulfilled prophecy by "baptizing in the desert region and preaching a baptism of repentance for the forgiveness of sins" (Mark 1:1-4). Matthew stresses the eschatological element in John's message, "Repent, for the kingdom of heaven is near" (Matt 3:1), and includes John's rebuke when he saw many of the Pharisees and Sadducees coming to him: "You brood of vipers! Who warned you to flee from the coming wrath? Produce fruit in keeping with repentance" (Matt 3:7-8). We see that "two of the most prominent and characteristic features of the Baptist's message are the note of apocalyptic judgement and the linking of baptism with a new moral life" (Flemington 1948:15).

It is quite possible that John's baptism had its roots in Jewish lustration rites. There were many Jews before John who had seen the inner meaning of external rites. Perhaps John, who came from a priestly family, learned the deeper meaning of lustrations and applied this insight in his ministry.

It seems more likely, however, that rootage for John's baptism is to be sought in the Qumran community. The location of John's baptism, the "Desert of Judea" (Matt 3:1), or, as Luke puts it, "the country around the Jordan" (Luke 3:3), was, according to Beasley-Murray, "the area north west of the Dead Sea and the Jordan Valley; that is, the area of the Qumran sect and the Jordan baptizers!" (1962:39).

Whether John was himself an Essene who lived for a time in the Qumran community, as some would suggest, is also a matter of conjecture. However, he must have known of their existence. He could not have been ignorant of their use of lustrations as a means of moral and religious cleansing, when combined with repentance. He could not have been ignorant of their eschatological expectations and of the perception of themselves as preparers of the way of the Lord. In fact, Isaiah 40:3, which Matthew 3:3 applies to John is "also the passage cited by those living in the Qumran community as applying to themselves" (Myers 1986:30). Apparently, what John did was to transform basic Qumran ideas and practices and use them in his own prophetic ministry for more radical and inclusive purposes.

As Beasley-Murray sees it,

> Everything in John's practice and preaching was more radical than that of the Covenanters: the eschatological expectation was more immediate; the call to repentance was more urgent; it was expressed in a once-for-all baptism; the message of warning and offer of the Kingdom hope was addressed to the whole nation and not to a privileged few—hence John could not be contained within a cloister. It is clear, therefore, that John did not take over the ideas of the sectaries of Qumran and the Jordan valley without modification; on the contrary he transformed whatever he adopted. Yet that he *did* receive a basis on which to work seems indubitable. John was indebted to the sectaries for raw material hard to come by elsewhere (1962:40).

Moreover, John's baptism may have had roots in a phenomenon known as "prophetic symbolism." According to H. Wheeler Robinson, prophetic symbolism refers to the "whole series of acts performed by the prophets in connection with, yet in relative independence of, their oral prophecies" (1942:131). According to Robinson, such actions as "Isaiah's walking about Jerusalem half-clad and barefoot" or the "enactment of the siege of Jerusalem by Ezekiel" were not mere "illustrations" or "symbolic magic." Nor do they in any way "contain God." Rather, the "prophetic act, by being in miniature or fragmentary form that which God will accomplish, becomes part of the means through which God will bring it about. . . . they are performed at His command in order to achieve, or help to achieve His own purpose" (1942:131-133).

There is no doubt that John regarded his work as prophetic, as a fulfillment of Isaiah's prophecy (Isa 40:3; John 1:23). It is likely that his baptism had rootage in prophetic symbolism so that we can conclude with Gilmore by saying that "John the Baptist stands in the prophetic tradition and that his symbolism approximates in most respects to that practiced by his predecessors" (1959:81).

Perhaps this survey of John's baptism can best be understood as follows:

> The uniqueness of his baptism was bound up with the uniqueness of his vocation. In him the age-long traditions of ritual lustrations combined with prophetic anticipations of judgement and redemption and found a medium in the ablutions of men that looked for redemption in Israel. The success of the instrument was greater than he could have dreamed: to it the Messiah himself submitted, then invested it with power for the community of the Kingdom (Beasley-Murray 1962:44).

Thus, we may summarize our study of Christian baptism's antecedents by saying that the "instrument" to which the Messiah "submitted" and which He "invested with power for the community of the Kingdom" was baptism. But baptism as a ritual form was an inheritance from the past. Its antecedents included: ancient non-Jewish lustrations; lustrations in the Old Testament; Jewish proselyte baptism; baptisms of the Qumran community; and the baptism of John the Baptist. Hence, Christian baptism did not begin in a vacuum. As a religious form it had a long and meaningful history.

With this study of its antecedents in mind, we shall now turn to a study of Christian baptism itself.

Christian Baptism: Symbol or Sacrament?

Some scholars have regarded Christian baptism as a ritual symbol and nothing more. E.K. Simpson, for example, wrote:

> That baptism has a symbolic reference to cleansing we do not deny; but a spiritual economy cannot be tied to a material agency as an indispensable channel of grace. How can a sign engross the virtue of the thing signified? (1954:115).

A similar view was taken by Jewett who, defending the "evangelical view of baptismal efficacy," asserted that "the outward rite is best understood . . . as a cognitive-symbolic one rather than a causative-sacramental one" (1978:4). This view also is usually taken by Baptists who "came to see baptism as nothing more than a beautiful picture of the change which comes in the individual's life when he is converted to Christ" (Donald Bridge and David Phypers 1977:26). It was also held by various Anabaptist groups, by many Protestant churches and by most Evangelicals, who would concur with the following item in the Trinity Evangelical Divinity School Statement of Faith: "We believe that water baptism and the Lord's Supper are ordinances to be observed by the Church during the present age. They are, however, not to be regarded as means of salvation" (1998:1).

Jack W. Cottrell, on the other hand, sees the "cognitive-symbolic" view of baptism as differing from the "Biblical consensus in several crucial respects" and affirms that it "originated in the sixteenth century in the mind of Huldreich Zwingli" (1990:35). Cottrell points out that during the previous 1500 years of the existence of the church, there was in theology and practice an agreement that baptism is more than a cognitive symbol. He emphasizes that Zwingli not only rejected the "*ex opere operato* concept" of baptism (which was not usually what earlier theologians believed), but that he also rejected the concept that God alone saves "via the blood of Christ and the Holy Spirit, with baptism being either the means or occasion of

God's working" (which is what earlier theologians usually did believe).[3] Beasley-Murray concluded that "the understanding of baptism as 'a beautiful and expressive symbol' *and nothing more* is irreconcilable with the New Testament" (1966:32). He granted that the Apostolic writers used symbolism in connection with "baptismal action," but he affirmed that they "go further and view the act as a symbol with power, that is, a sacrament" (1962:263).

Which View Is Correct?

Is Christian baptism a purely symbolic ritual or is it also a sacrament? Which of these opposing views is correct?

To answer this question, I shall study both the general phenomenon of ritual symbolism and also the symbolisms expressed in particular by the ritual of Christian baptism. Then, I shall investigate the definitions, purposes and efficacy of sacraments. In particular, I shall study whether Christian baptism is, indeed, a sacrament and, if so, what happens during its enactment or what is effected by it.

Ritual Symbolism

Mary Douglas begins her book, *Natural Symbols,* with the following assertion:

> "One of the gravest problems of our day is the lack of commitment to common symbols. . . . a wide-spread, explicit rejection of rituals as such. Ritual has become a bad word signifying empty conformity. We are witnessing a revolt against formalism, even form . . . We find ourselves, here and now, reliving a worldwide revolt against ritualism" (1970:19).

We do, indeed, live during a time when it is popular to oppose form and ceremony, perhaps even a time when there is "a wide-spread, explicit rejection of rituals as such."

Greetings as Ritual Symbolism

Yet, those who revolt against forms, rituals and ceremonies use rituals every day, often unaware that they are doing so. For example, as Thomas Howard points out,

> We shake hands. Nothing is gained by this, at least nothing utilitarian. It is pure ceremony. Here come two primates pell-mell on the business of the day. As they approach one another, each extends an extremity and they interlace briefly. Neither of them needed an assist over a mud puddle or help with a heavy package. Nothing appears to have been gained by this. If we were to ask them what they were about, they would say, "We were shaking hands." Shaking hands? *Shaking hands?* What has that got to do with anything? What about wiggling toes? We don't understand what you brought about by the act. Do you do it every time? Or can you decide on the spur of the moment what dance you will do? No, no, we are told; it's just what people *do*. It doesn't accomplish anything. It's just what we do. . . . Presumably an anthropologist or historian might tell us the cultural origins of the handshake, and in those origins there might be observable some function. But whatever the function was, it has long since ceased to operate as that function, and exists as a ritual residue. . . . It is as good a way as any of saying a great deal without wasting time going through verbal protestations of honor (1969:40-41).

But, even when we use *words* of greeting instead of, or in addition to, the handshake, we use ordinary words in a special or extraordinary sense. Paul G. Hiebert calls such special word usage "bracketing" and views our standard verbal greetings as ritual. Hiebert thinks of ritual as "a collection of symbols in an organized form" and recognizes that, in our greetings, we have a standard set of responses:

> "Hello. — Hello. How are you? — Just fine, and you? O.K. Things are hectic, you know. — They sure are . . . (and so on)." If we take these responses at face value, they often appear to be hypocritical. "How are you? — Just fine." In

fact, we are feeling terrible, our bank account is overdrawn, and we are caught in a tangle at work. Nevertheless, we say, "Just fine!" The reason is, the ritual does not refer to our personal state of affairs. It speaks to the state of the relationship between us. When we say, "Just fine," we are saying that the relationship between us is going well. We recognize and appreciate the other person. (1986:5).

Thus those who use handshakes and the standard verbal greetings use ritual, even though they may not be aware of it.

Other Symbolic Rituals

The same thing happens when we set the table for a meal. What is going on? We are trying to get food from point A (the garden or the shelf or the stove) to point B (our stomach). We could do this transfer of food in a barnyard way with a trough or even more efficiently with injections. Instead, at least in Western cultures most of the time, we set the table and raise the function of eating to elaborate heights by ritualizing it (Howard 1969:41).

The same tendency to move through experience ceremonially or ritualistically is seen in the fact that we have a funeral for the burial of the dead. What is going on during a funeral? Can we actually *do* anything for the deceased? No. But we cannot leave the grief, the awe, the silence, the perplexity, the ruin just flying around in a windy clutter. There is no question of disposing of the body like refuse with the trash. We take the whole experience and move through it ritualistically. There is a funeral ceremony (1969:46-53).

Ritual Symbolism: A Mark of Humanness

These reflections remind us that humans use ritual symbolism not just at weddings, banquets, presidential inaugurations, graduations, Independence Day celebrations and in corporate worship. Instead, Howard asserts, "we are the sort of creatures who have ceremonialized nearly everything we do" (1976:62). Hence, it may not be accurate to call those who are in explicit revolt against rituals "non-ritualists," for it is difficult for anyone to get through a day spent in human society without doing something ritually (handshakes, verbal greetings, waving to a friend, opening a door for a lady, setting a table for a meal). Thus, those who revolt against ritualism use rituals regularly. And even those Christians who have a lot to say against "the same old forms and rituals all the time" usually do not desire to do away with all Christian ritual or even think a "ritualless" Christianity possible. Instead, it is usually held that we need new rituals or that we need to use the old rituals in a more meaningful manner or both.

In my own case, I have come to regard form, ritual and ceremony as very important, even essential, aspects of what it means to be human. I have come to agree with Howard's assessment that

> We are ceremonial creatures.
> To see this we need only recall a very simple thing. The more important an event or experience is for us mortals, the more we ceremonialize it. We may take the three most basic experiences of human life as illustrations: birth, mating, and death. We, like dogs, pass through all of these, but unlike dogs, we are not content merely to pass through them; we must also *do something about them*. This seems to be the mark of our humaness [sic], and the thing we do about these experiences is to ceremonialize them. All of them are routine, but we, being human and not merely bestial, see something in them. We see significance, and the thing we do about significance is to reach for ceremony (1984:97).

Anthropological Study of Rituals

The school of symbolic anthropology of Mary Douglas, Clifford Geertz, Nancy Munn, David Schneider, Terence Turner, Victor Turner, and others, although not in agreement on all points, is in fundamental agreement with Howard's assessment.[4] These scholars see culture as "primarily a system of symbols" (L.L. Langness 1974:117). They emphasize the relationship between "symbolic form and cultural meaning" (Munn 1973:581). And they stress that complex multiple meanings can be built into ritual symbolism (V. Turner 1967:284-285).

This survey of the importance of ritual symbolism has mentioned several different symbolic rituals. Some are as simple as shaking hands or standard verbal greetings. Some are as complicated as funeral rites or wedding ceremonies. Such rituals are, to use V. Turner's phrase, "multivocal or polysemous" (1967:284). Whether "simple" or "complicated," there is a density of significance built into actions of ritual symbolism which puts a "multiplicity of meanings into social circulation in managable form" (Munn 1973:592).

Christian Baptism as Ritual Symbolism

If we accept Munn and V. Turner's views about the complexity of multiple meanings which are built into ritual symbolism, we would expect to find "multivocality" evident in Christian baptism and suspect that undue emphasis on only one or two of this ritual symbol's possible meanings would lead to a truncated view of the rite. Is this actually the case? Let us turn now to the evidence in the New Testament to study the symbolisms that are carried by baptism according to the original teachers and practitioners of this Christian rite.

Washing

According to Vernard Eller, "There is plenty of New Testament evidence to indicate that 'washing' is one of the symbolisms carried by baptism" (1972:46).

References familiar to New Testament students follow:

And now what are you waiting for? Get up, be baptized and wash your sins away, calling on his name (Acts 22:16).

But you were washed, you were sanctified, you were justified in the name of the Lord Jesus Christ and by the Spirit of our God (1 Cor 6:11).

He saved us through the washing of rebirth and renewal by the Holy Spirit (Titus 3:5).

Christ loved the church . . . cleansing her by the washing with water through the word (Eph 5:25-26).

. . . let us draw near to God with a sincere heart in full assurance of faith, having our hearts sprinkled to cleanse us from a guilty conscience and having our bodies washed with pure water (Heb 10:22).

Although we cannot be certain that the last two citations refer to baptism, it is quite possible that they do. In my view, the first three clearly refer to baptism.

The first three citations also clearly associate forgiveness with the washing of baptism. This is the first way in which Christian baptism differs from various Old Testament lustrations for, as Eller points out, "forgiveness invariably assumes a close, personal, two-way relationship between the sinner and God. God does the forgiving, yes; but man must repent and allow himself to be forgiven" (1972:47). But the ritual washings of the Old Testament do not carry such personal "two-way relationship" overtones. Moreover, Christian baptism was not a repeated washing that was to be done time after time after time. Rather, it had a once-for-all aspect which gave it "an eschatological, an end-state, orientation that the repeated washings did not possess" (Eller 1972:48).

Hence, although Christian baptism does differ in significant ways from its antecedents in Jewish lustration rites, it did carry forward the symbolism of the washing of forgiveness.

Death, Burial and Resurrection with Christ

The symbolism of death, burial and resurrection with Christ carried by Christian baptism is especially stressed in Romans 6:1-4 and in Colossians 2:12. In the relevant clauses Paul asserts that those who were "baptized into Christ Jesus were baptized into his death" (Rom 6:3) and that "just as Christ was raised from the dead . . . we too may live a new life" (Rom 6:4). Paul wrote of the Colossian Christians as those who "have been given fullness in Christ . . . having been buried with him in baptism and raised with him through your faith in the power of God, who raised him from the dead (Col 2:10a,12).

Thus baptism symbolized the burial of those who "died to sin" (Rom 6:2). It symbolized the burial of those who entered "into Christ Jesus . . . into his death" (Rom 6:3). It also symbolized a resurrection with Christ that "we too may live a new life" (Rom 6:4) by the "power of God, who raised him from the dead" (Col 2:12).

Reclothing

You are all sons of God through faith in Christ Jesus, for all of you who were baptized into Christ have clothed yourselves with Christ (Gal 3:26-27).

The symbol of reclothing to represent a spiritual change is familiar to students of the Old Testament. Isaiah called on Jerusalem to "awake" and "put on your garments of splendor" (Isa 52:1). He pictured the day of rebuilding, restoration and renewal as the day of reclothing with "garments of salvation" and a "robe of righteousness" (Isa 61:10). Zechariah also used reclothing symbolism in his story of clean garments for the high priest, Joshua:

Now Joshua was dressed in filthy clothes as he stood before the angel. The angel said to those who were standing before him, "Take off his filthy clothes."

Then he said to Joshua, "See, I have taken away your sin,
and I will put rich garments on you" (Zech 3:3-4).

The symbolism of spiritual reclothing is carried forward
into New Testament teaching and into the practice of Christian
baptism. The key idea is that those who were baptized into
Christ were reclothed with Christ, as Paul reminded the
Galatian Christians, "for all of you who were baptized into
Christ have clothed yourselves with Christ" (Gal 3:27). They
were dressed with Him, not in the "filthy clothes" of their old
life of sin. The baptized ones have stripped off an old life and
put on a new one. They have "taken off" an "old self with its
practices" and have "put on the new self, which is being renewed
. . . in the image of its Creator" (Col 3:9-10). They have taken
off their "filthy clothes" and have been reclothed in "garments
of splendor," "garments of salvation," with Christ Himself, the
ultimate "robe of righteousness."

Incorporation

Romans 6:3 and Galatians 3:27 both teach that early
Christians had been "baptized into Christ." Early Christians
"were all baptized by one Spirit into one body . . ." (1 Cor
12:13). When Peter concluded his sermon on Pentecost, "Those
who accepted his message were baptized, and about three thousand were added to their number that day" (Acts 2:41).

Concerning what happened on Pentecost, Beasley-Murray
commented, "Apart from an explicit statement, words could
hardly have expressed more clearly the conviction that by
baptism the convert forsakes the Israel that had rejected the
Messiah, to join the community that owned His sovereignty"
(1962:104). Flemington, in a similar vein, commented that
"for the overwhelming majority of early Christians, baptism
with water, from the day of Pentecost onwards, was recognized
and practiced as the accepted mode of admission into the new
community" (1948:116). Still speaking of Christian baptism,

Flemington adds: "The rite was conceived realistically as the typical means whereby the believer was incorporated into the Body of Christ. To be baptized 'into Christ,' and to be baptized into that Body of Christ which was the new Israel, were one and the same experience" (1948:126). Thus Christian baptism symbolized the believer's incorporation into Christ and His spiritual body, the church. According to Donald Baillie, this is a "principle which is accepted by all churches . . . that *baptism marks the entry of the individual into the community of the church of Christ on earth*" (1957:80).

New Birth

The symbolism of baptism as "new birth" or being "born again" is prominent in Jesus' conversation with Nicodemus. "'How can a man be born when he is old?' Nicodemus asked. 'Surely he cannot enter a second time into his mother's womb to be born!' Jesus answered, 'I tell you the truth, no one can enter the kingdom of God unless he is born of water and the Spirit'" (John 3:4-5). What Jesus said to Nicodemus must have struck him like a blow. Jesus calmly told him that he was not yet in the kingdom. Nicodemus must be born again — not another physical birth, but a spiritual birth, a birth wrought by the Holy Spirit. It is a work of God. It is not a matter of human merit. Yet, it is a birth of water as well as of Spirit.[5] Although we must not suppose that every mention of water in John refers to baptism, I think it is correct to conclude that "at a time when the employment of water for cleansing in view of the last day had taken the specific form of baptism, it is difficult to take seriously any other references than baptism in the words ἐξ ὕδατος [*ex hydatos*]" (Beasley-Murray 1962:228). Interpreted in this manner, Christian baptism symbolizes the new birth.

Baptism Was Ritual Symbolism

Hence, those scholars who view Christian baptism as a "beautiful and expressive symbol" are correct. The New Testament does present Christian baptism as a ritual symbol which was viewed as: a washing of forgiveness (Acts 22:16; 1 Cor 6:11; Titus 3:5); a participation in and a reenactment of the death, burial and resurrection of Christ (Rom 6:1-4; Col 2:11-14); a reclothing with Christ (Gal 3:26-27); an incorporation into Christ and His body, the church (Acts 2:41; Rom 6:3; 1 Cor 12:13; Gal 3:26-27) and a new birth (John 3:4-5). Thus there was a "multivocality" and a complexity of meaning carried by Christian baptism in the New Testament which would lead one not only to declare it to be a "beautiful and expressive symbol" or to say it was "cognitive-symbolic" but which would also lead one to see it as a reenactment, an adumbration or an icon of the gospel itself. As Flemington expressed it, "It is clear that for the earliest disciples baptism in some vivid way connotated and 'symbolized' the Gospel message. It was what might be called an embodiment of the *kerygma*" (1948:49). There is no doubt, then, that baptism was a symbol, even a ritual, "a collection of symbols in organized form" (Hiebert 1986:5).

Beyond Ritual Symbolism?

' But are those who view Christian baptism as a "beautiful and expressive symbol" *and nothing more* correct? Are they correct to see Christian baptism merely as ritual symbolism? Was it more than that to the earliest Christians? Is it possible that Christian baptism was a sacrament, a "symbol with power," as Beasley-Murray defines it (1962:263)?

Christian Baptism as Sacrament

We shall now turn to study this more controversial aspect of our topic. We shall study whether Christian baptism was a sacrament, and, if so, what happened during it or what was effected by it.

Definitions

To decide whether Christian baptism was a sacrament one needs to answer the obvious question, "What is a sacrament?" We shall now attempt a comprehensive definition.

Etymology

The term "sacrament" is not a Biblical word.[6] "In the Gr NT . . . there is no word . . . corresponding to 'sacrament,' . . . [even though] it had been employed to translate the Gr μυστή–ριον, *musterion*, 'a mystery'" (J.C. Lambert 1952:2636). Instead, a study of the etymology of the word "sacrament" reveals that it

> comes from the Lat *sacramentum*, which in the classical period of the language was used in two chief senses: (1) as a legal term to denote the sum of money deposited by two parties to a suit which was forfeited by the loser and appropriated to sacred uses; (2) as a military term to designate the oath of obedience taken by newly enlisted soldiers (Lambert 1952:2636).

Whether viewed as an "oath of obedience" or as something "appropriated to sacred uses," it is apparent that *sacramentum* could readily be used to describe such ritual symbols as baptism and the Lord's Supper.

Historical Development

Actually, the term "sacrament" has been applied during the history of the church far beyond its references to baptism and the Lord's Supper, even beyond its references to the seven traditional sacraments of Roman Catholicism.[7] Used in the broadest sense, the word "sacrament" has "been applied generally to all kinds of signs or actions with a certain spiritual significance," and has even been extended to "cover all the material things which speak to us of God and His actions, so that ultimately the universe itself may be regarded as sacramental by the Christian" (G.W. Bromiley 1957:12).

According to Robert Webber, the church fathers saw many things as sacramental because they recognized many means by which Christ's saving reality was signified. Tertullian, for example,

> went back to the Old Testament and saw sacramental signs everywhere: the Exodus is sacramental because it points to the Christ event; the offices of prophet, priest, and king are sacramental because they are fulfilled in Christ, . . . Even the Tabernacle and the Temple, with all their sacrifices and sacred rituals, were seen as sacramental. . . . [because] these visible, tangible, and concrete realities . . . looked to Jesus, the person whose reality they signified (1985:48-49).

Although Augustine's definition of a sacrament as "the visible form of an invisible grace" limited its application, we see how far even this idea may be stretched when "we find Hugo of St. Victor (12th cent.) enumerating as many as 30 sacraments that had been recognized in the church" (Lambert 1952:2636).

As is well known, Western churches finally decided to delimit the term, the Roman Catholic Church fixing the number at the traditional seven and many Protestant churches recognizing only two: baptism and the Lord's Supper.[8] It is this more precise or specific usage of the term that concerns us when we ask whether Christian baptism was a sacrament in New Testament teaching and practice. What is a sacrament in this more precise sense?

More Precise Definitions

According to Hugo of St. Victor a sacrament is a "physical or material element presented clearly to the senses, by similitude representing, by institution signifying, and by consecration containing an invisible and spiritual grace" (Kenneth Scott Latourette 1975:505). According to Thomas Aquinas, a sacrament is "the sign of a sacred thing in so far as it sanctifies men" (F.L. Cross 1957:1198). John Calvin defined a sacrament as

> an external sign by which the Lord seals on our consciences His promises of good-will toward us in order to sustain the weakness of our faith, and we in turn testify our piety toward Him, both before Himself, and before angels as well as men (*Institutes*, IV, xvi,21).[9]

Baillie viewed a sacrament as a "sensible sign" which is "an instrument of divine grace" (1957:49). W. Bousset thought of a sacrament as "a sacred action in which a supernatural grace is imparted to the believer through material means" (1926:199). Webber stresses that "the sacrament is not a thing in itself, an end, but a means through which Christ encounters us savingly" (1985:50-51).

The "sensible signs" of a sacrament which are instrumental or efficacious to the believer's receiving divine grace do not consist, according to Baillie, "only of the elements . . . but also of *the actions*, including the words spoken; but neither the words nor the elements as apart from the actions" (1957:94). The definition of the Catechism of *The Book of Common Prayer* is meaningful and comprehensive. According to this widely accepted document, a sacrament is

> an outward and visible sign of an inward and spiritual grace given unto us; ordained by Christ himself, as a means whereby we receive the same and a pledge to assure us thereof (Church of England 1662:294).

These definitions present what Michael Anderson calls "the notion of sacrament — that material things could be instruments of grace, vehicles of the Divine" (1985:94).

Hence, when we ask whether baptism is a sacrament, we are basically asking whether baptism is an instrument or a means through which we receive divine grace. We are asking whether baptism is an "efficacious sign."

Why Use Sacraments?

But do we need efficacious signs? Do we need sacraments? Why should we not be content with the merely cognitive, rational elements in our faith? Why should we not be content to permit our spirits to communicate directly with His Spirit in Christian conversion and worship? Why do we need sensible signs or material means?

I think Calvin's view of this was correct. He thought that "God in His wonderful providence has accommodated Himself to our capacity, because in this mortal life we are not purely spiritual beings like angels, but live in bodies of flesh" (Baillie 1957:87).[10] By using sacraments, "material things" as "instruments of grace," God is accommodating Himself to the realities of our composite natures, our pneumo-psycho-somatic natures. We are not solely spiritual or merely mental beings. Our composite natures include biochemical, material bodies as well, and God uses these "visible, tangible . . . material things and . . . perceptible actions which we call sacramental" (Baillie 1957:42) because they are suitable to our present condition.

This should not surprise us since the central belief of the Christian faith is that "the Word became flesh" (John 1:14). God took on a body of flesh, died a physical death and experienced a bodily resurrection for our salvation (1 Cor 15:1-4). The sacraments mirror that reality. The sacraments are as "visible and corporeal as was the life of Jesus in the flesh" (Baillie 1957:61). If our faith were merely a system of abstract truth not rooted in the historical Incarnation, we might devise many different symbolic rites suited to different cultures and times. Instead, we have an historical gospel. We believe in salvation through the actual death, burial and resurrection of God Incarnate. The Lord's Supper and baptism have redemptive rootage right back into that. They have "an integral continuity with the incarnation" (Baillie 1957:60). As Anderson puts it, "the worship of an incarnate God required a corresponding carnality" (1985:95).

How Do Sacraments Work?

But, if we grant our need for sacraments and if we grant that a sacrament is an "efficacious sign," this raises the further question of the efficacy of sacraments. How do they work? Even among churches which are "sacramental," explanations of sacramental efficacy differ. The Roman Catholic view stresses a power inherent in the sacraments themselves, the Reformed view stresses the blessing of Christ and His Spirit conditioned by the receiver's faith, and the Lutheran position affirms both the power inherent in the sacraments and the necessity of the receiver's faith but views the power of the elements and actions of the sacraments not as inherent but due to their embodiment of the Divine word.[11]

But such a summary paints with a broad brush. In the popular sense of the phrase, *ex opere operato* (the Roman Catholic view) approximates something "magical." The popular view, however, forgets that the scholastic formula

> in its full form is *ex opere operato non opponentibus obicem*, and that the second half of the formula is of equal validity with the first. It is possible by interposing an obstacle to render the external act ineffective and deprive it of its spiritual value. All sacramental acts require for their efficacy the right dispositions in the recipient (H. Balmforth 1937:46).

Hence, the Roman Catholic view is not "magical," but includes the disposition of recipients. Moreover, the Reformed view

> saw that there can be no isolation of the sign from its meaning. But it has always been realized that baptism . . . is more than an eloquent action. It is also an effective action. It does not merely attest the grace of God. It is itself, in the Holy Spirit, a means of grace. If it can be called a sign, it

must also be called an effective sign, something which God has instituted in order that He may achieve certain results through it (Bromiley 1957:28-29).

The Reformed view while not including *ex opere operato*, sees baptism, nevertheless, as a "means of grace." And the Lutheran view, while not stressing the Holy Spirit as much as the Reformed view, does stress the Divine word's presence and power in the sacraments.

Christian Baptism as Sacrament

We are now better prepared to ask whether Christian baptism is a sacrament. To ask this question is to ask whether Christian baptism is a "means" or an "instrument of divine grace." It is to ask whether Christian baptism is an "efficacious" sign in human salvation.

In light of the foregoing study, my reply is, "Yes." Christian baptism as presented in the New Testament and practiced by the early Christians was a sacrament. I define sacrament as a means or a channel of divine grace. In my view, a sacrament is a visible sign through which God grants the benefits symbolized by the ritual. I regard baptism as a sacrament, a symbol with power. But the power is neither in the water nor in the action of baptism *per se*. Rather, the power is God's power. As I see it, baptism is an efficacious sign, but the efficacy is not in baptism itself, but in God's gracious action.

I agree with Bromiley that baptism is more than "an eloquent action. It is an effective action" (1957:29). I concur with Beasley-Murray that "the understanding of baptism as 'a beautiful and expressive symbol,' *and nothing more*, is irreconcilable with the New Testament" (1966:32). I accept Flemington's conclusion that "in Christian baptism something is not merely expressed but actually accomplished" (1948:80).

I do not agree with the view which Jewett attributes to those who espouse what he calls "sacramental theology."

According to Jewett, this view "regards this view as inherently efficacious to mediate the inward grace (blessing) of which they are the outward sign" (1978:3). I do not think that baptism is "inherently efficacious to mediate . . . grace." As I understand the sacrament of baptism, it has no power *per se*. It "regenerates" no one. It is not magical. Instead, it is God Himself, by the Spirit, who acts. It is God Himself who saves, who regenerates. God Himself does this on the occasion of the baptism of a penitent believer. Baptism is the "sacrament that unites the individual, through faith that reaches up from the heart, with the grace of God, which in turn reaches down" (Gilliland 1983:90) in the experience of conversion. Hence, as David W. Fletcher expresses it, baptism is a "true means of grace for those who receive it in faith. The thing signified by baptism, i.e., washing away of sins in the blood of Christ, is actually bestowed at point of baptism. It is not only a sign, but a true means" (1990:10). Baptism is the means God uses. It is the sacrament of conversion.

Baptism as Ordinance: A Helpful Middle Position?

At this point a careful student might ask, "But are these the only two choices? Must we choose between sacrament and ritual symbol? Isn't it more helpful to take a middle position and refer to baptism as an ordinance?" To which I respond, of course baptism is an ordinance. It is an ordinance of Christ. It is a Dominical ordinance. Christ Himself ordained, decreed, mandated baptism (Matt 28:19). But stressing baptism as ordinance is not the solution we search for. Why not? Because, either way, baptism is an ordinance. If Christian baptism is a mere symbol, just a beautiful picture of what has already occurred prior to baptism, it is, nevertheless, a symbol which Christ decreed or ordained. Viewed like this, baptism could be called a *symbolic ordinance*. On the other hand, if baptism is a sacrament, an "efficacious" sign or an "instrument of divine grace," it is, nevertheless, a sacrament which Christ decreed or ordained. Viewed like this, baptism could be called a *sacramental ordinance*. But, either way, it is still an *ordinance*, and the question as to whether baptism is merely a symbol or also a sacrament still remains. Emphasizing that baptism is an ordinance, ordained by Christ Himself, is proper and therefore helpful. But such an emphasis does not solve the problem with which we have struggled. The proper solution, in my view, is to regard baptism as the sacrament — or if you prefer, the sacramental ordinance — of conversion.

Beyond Ritual Symbolism

To say that Christian baptism is a sacrament takes us beyond ritual symbolism. It even takes us beyond viewing baptism as an adumbration, icon or embodiment of the gospel, although it includes all that. It is important to note, however, that if baptism did not include ritual symbolism, it would not take us beyond it. As Baillie put it,

> Every school of theological thought, and every Church, speaks of [a] sacrament as a 'sensible sign' or a symbol. This is not to say that the sacraments are *merely* signs or symbols. They are more. But if they were not signs, they could not be more. It is through being signs, through their symbolism, that they come to be more (1957:93).

The Efficacy of Christian Baptism

If baptism is a sacrament, something is accomplished or effected through it. But what? What is it that happens or is brought about through this sacrament? Based on the foregoing study, I conclude that *what is symbolized by the ritual of Christian baptism God also effects through it.* Christian baptism in the New Testament symbolized: a washing of forgiveness; a participation in the death, burial and resurrection of Christ; a reclothing with Christ; an incorporation into Christ and His body, and a new birth. I conclude that these benefits symbolized by baptism are the benefits God gives through it. Such expressions as "be baptized and wash your sins away" (Acts 22:16), "baptized into Christ Jesus . . . baptized into his death" (Rom 6:3), "you who were baptized into Christ have clothed yourselves with Christ" (Gal 3:26-27), "we were all baptized by one Spirit into one body" (1 Cor 12:13), and "no one can enter the kingdom of God unless he is born of water and the Spirit" (John 3:5) lead to this conclusion. Moreover, Peter's command on Pentecost, "Repent and be baptized, every one of you, in the name of Jesus Christ for the forgiveness of your sins" (Acts 2:38) and his assertion that "baptism . . . now saves you also" (1 Pet 3:21) are difficult to comprehend on any terms other than sacramental.[12]

Back of all this, of course, is the Dominical mandate, "Therefore go and make disciples of all nations, baptizing them in the name of the Father and of the Son and of the Holy Spirit" (Matt 28:19). According to White, if baptism is a mere symbol *and nothing more*, "the claim to dominical authority becomes inexplicable." He then asks, "Did Jesus really require of His followers a religious exercise merely symbolic, devoid of profit, efficacy or result?" (1960:306). One may logically conclude that He did not require a merely symbolic exercise devoid of efficacy. Instead, He and His apostles required a sacrament through which He Himself would give the benefits symbolized by the rite which was the sign of the sacrament.

God's Saving Action

It is God Himself who saves us in the sacrament of baptism. Salvation is not basically a human, but a divine action. Beasley-Murray expressed this idea as follows:

> Schnackenburg insists on the necessity to hold together symbol and effect in the sacrament, and also to realize that the sole effect that can be present in a sacrament is the saving

action of God Himself. "Baptism is not a human manipulation, a secret procedure through which a man may appropriate something hard to obtain. The blessings of salvation
mediated through it are bestowed by God" (1966:22-23).

White stressed God's primacy in the sacrament of baptism
when he wrote:

> We may speak of Paul's sacramentalism, provided we
> remember that to his mind efficacy belongs not to the cere-
> mony of baptism as such but to the action of God, by the
> Spirit, within the soul of the convert who at this time and in
> this way is making his response to the grace offered him in
> the gospel (1960:226).

Even though, in a baptismal context, Peter can plead, "Save yourselves from this corrupt generation" (Acts 2:40), this exhorta-
tion does not imply that salvation is basically from man, by his
merit or achievement. Rather, it refers to the human response
to salvation offered by God's grace.

Baptism or Faith: Which Saves?

Still, it is asked, "Are we saved by faith or by baptism?"
Baillie points out that this question poses a "false antithesis and
alternative. The truth is that we are [basically or ultimately]
saved by neither, but by God. But He saves us through faith,
and therefore partly through sacraments, which He uses to
awaken and strengthen our faith" (1957:101).

True, we are saved by faith. But saving faith in the New
Testament is not merely cognitive trust. Rather, it is faith which
"expresses itself" (Gal 5:6) or faith which is "accompanied by
action" (Jas 2:17). In that sense, salvation is "not by faith
alone" (Jas 2:24) but by faith which works or acts or expresses
itself as God requires. As White points out,

> Men are saved by faith: but faith . . . can degenerate into a
> transient mood of the soul unless it be given body, sub-

stance, objectivity, in the overt acts of believing men. Faith needs to be "objectified" in the sacramental experience of the believer, and this involves no inconsistency, because . . . "sacrament" *means* "faith-sacrament." There is no tension, dualism, or contradiction in requiring faith and sacrament, because baptism is believer's baptism . . . Tension arises when baptism [is] divorced from faith and then set over against it (1960:263-264).

Beasley-Murray demonstrated that we must not divorce baptism from faith or set baptism over against faith. He decided that "it might be profitable to tabulate the associations of baptism in the New Testament writings and those of faith, and see to what extent there was a correlation between the two" (1966:27). What he found was that the following "blessings" or "gifts" are associated with both baptism *and* faith: forgiveness of sins, union with Christ, possession of the Spirit, membership in the church, and inheritance of the Kingdom of God (1966:27-30). From these New Testament statements about baptism and faith he concluded that

God's gift to baptism and to faith is one: It is his salvation in Christ. There is no question of his giving one part in baptism and another to faith, whether in that order or in the reverse. He gives *all* in baptism and *all* to faith. From this I find an inescapable conclusion: God's gracious giving to faith belongs to the context of baptism, even as God's gracious giving in baptism is to faith. Faith has no merit to claim such gifts and baptism has no power to produce them. It is all of God, who brings a man to faith and to baptism and has been pleased to so order his giving (1966:37).

Five Components of New Testament Conversion

Robert H. Stein, taking a similar approach, has investigated "how baptism is related to the experience of conversion in the New Testament." His thesis is as follows:

In the New Testament, conversion involves five integrally related components or aspects, all of which took place at the same time, usually on the same day. These five components are repentance, faith, and confession by the individual, regeneration, or the giving of the Holy Spirit by God, and baptism by representatives of the Christian community (1998:6).

Stein thinks that this thesis is "able to explain the majority of the New Testament evidence quite well." He seeks to "prove" his thesis in three ways.

First, I shall demonstrate that the New Testament presents these five elements in various combinations as being intimately interrelated and as occurring at the same time, so that we should assume that they belonged together. Second, I shall demonstrate that different components are singled out as bringing about the same result. Third, I shall present a hypothetical situation involving a first-century Christian to see if this thesis makes sense both with regard to the New Testament materials and to the experience of the earliest Christians (1998:6).

According to Stein, "It seems clear by the varied groupings of these aspects in the New Testament that the experience of conversion was understood to involve all five components which normally occurred at the same time." He then lists the following "combinations" as "associated together" in conversion: "Faith and Baptism" (Gal 3:26-27); "Repentance and Baptism" (Acts 2:38; 11:15-18); "Faith and Regeneration" (Gal 3:2; Eph 1:3); "Baptism and Regeneration" (Titus 3:4-5); "Faith and Confession" (Rom 10:9); "Baptism and Confession" (Acts 22:16); "Faith and Repentance" (Mark 1:14-15; Acts 20:21); "Repentance, Baptism and Regeneration" (Acts 2:37-38; 11:1-18); "Faith, Baptism, Regeneration, and Repentance" (Acts 19:1-6; 2:38).

In view of these elements which are associated in various combinations in the New Testament, Stein concludes that

all five of these components (repentance, faith, confession,
regeneration, and baptism) were understood by the biblical
writers to be involved in the conversion experience. *They are
inseparable.* At times one or more of them may be omitted,
according to the emphasis of the writer, but even if a component is not mentioned it is nevertheless implied and
assumed (1998:10, emphasis mine).

Then, in addition to assuming that these five elements belong
together as integral components of the conversion experience
because of the various ways in which they are associated, Stein
points out that these "different components produce the same
results. At various times different components of the conversion
experience are described as bringing about either salvation or justification" (1998:10). He then lists the following components
which bring about either salvation or justification (1998:11-12):
"Salvation Comes through Repentance" (2 Pet 3:9; 2 Cor 7:10);
"Salvation Comes through Faith" (Eph 2:8-9; Acts 16:31; John
3:16-17); "Salvation Comes through Confession" (Rom 10:9-
13); "Salvation Comes through Regeneration" (Titus 3:5; John
3:3,5); "Salvation Comes through Baptism" (1 Pet 3:21);
"Justification Comes through Faith" (Rom 3:28; 5:1; Gal 2:5);
"Justification Comes through Baptism" (1 Cor 6:11; Acts 2:38).
According to Stein, "all five components" noted in his thesis
"are mentioned in the New Testament as bringing about salvation. Rather than argue that each component is a different path
to salvation and that one could choose whichever path one liked
best, it appears simpler and more reasonable to assume that *all
five elements were present in the experience of conversion*" (1998:
11,12, emphasis mine).

   With reference to baptism, Stein says that 1 Pet 3:21, "and
this water symbolizes baptism that now saves you also," is a
verse "which is notoriously difficult for non-sacramentalists,"
because it "appears to say that salvation comes through baptism." But he views that passage as "quite understandable" if
baptism is seen as part of "a repentance-faith-confession-regen-
eration-baptism conversion." Viewed in this way, "interpreta-

tions which seek to deny the normal meaning of the term 'baptism' are not necessary" (1998:11).

To help us understand how this "makes sense both with regard to the New Testament materials and to the experience of the earliest Christians" (1998:6), Stein presents the following hypothetical interview with "Isaac of Antioch," a first century believer:

Monday, April 5, A.D. 49

Interviewer: "Isaac, do you remember the day when you were converted?"

Isaac: "Oh, yes, I remember clearly that Barnabas preached that I was a sinner. Yet because of Jesus Christ, if I would turn from my sin, God would forgive me. So, on August 15, A.D. 44, *I repented* of my sin and became a Christian.

Tuesday, April 6, A.D. 49

Interviewer: "Isaac, do you remember the day when you were converted?"

Isaac: "Oh, yes, I remember clearly that Barnabas preached that God had fulfilled the promises that he made to our fathers and sent his Messiah, Jesus Christ. So on August 15, A.D. 44, *I confessed* Jesus as the Messiah and Lord and became a Christian."

Wednesday, April 7, A.D. 49

Interviewer: "Isaac, do you remember the day when you were converted?"

Isaac: "Oh, yes, I remember clearly that Barnabas preached that I could not be saved by my own efforts, for all my works were as filthy rags. He said that I need to trust in the grace of God and simply believe the gospel because God had made salvation in Christ possible for me. So, on August 15, A.D. 44, *I trusted by faith* in the grace of God and became a Christian.

Thursday, April 8, A.D. 49

Interviewer: "Isaac, do you remember the day when you were converted?"

Isaac: "Oh, yes, I remember clearly that Barnabas preached

that I needed to be born again and that I should not marvel I needed to be made new by the Holy Spirit. So, on August 15, A.D. 44, *I was born again* through the Spirit of God and became a Christian."

Friday, April 9, A.D. 49

Interviewer: "Isaac, do you remember the day when you were converted?"

Isaac: "Oh, yes, I remember clearly that Barnabas preached that I needed to die, be buried with Christ, and be raised in newness of life. So, on August 15, A.D. 44, I was *baptized* in the name of the Lord Jesus Christ and became a Christian."

Interviewer: "Now Isaac, come on. You have told us five different stories. Which is the true one? When were you truly converted? When and how did you really become a Christian? Was it when you repented? When you believed? When you confessed Christ? When you were born again? Or was it when you were baptized?

How would Isaac respond to these questions? I believe that he would respond essentially as follows: "All these were involved and associated with my becoming a Christian. When Barnabas preached to me, he not only spoke of my being a sinner and needing to repent, but he also talked about my need to put my faith in Jesus Christ, confess him as Lord and Christ, be born of the Spirit, and be baptized. All these took place on August 15, A.D. 44. All five were involved in my conversion!" (1998:12-13).

Is Salvation by Sacramental Action Alone?

Salvation is not by baptism alone. Nor is it by faith alone. Rather salvation is by God's grace extended through the gospel which is embodied in baptism. Through his baptism as faith expressed, the new convert looks to God's power to perform what he promised. Baptism looks by faith to the grace of God for salvation. Baptism is an act of faith by which the sinner accepts what the power of God has done for him through the crucified-resurrected Christ, and it is also a sacrament through which God gives the benefits symbolized by the rite.

If this understanding of baptism is not correct, if Christian baptism is not a sacrament but merely a symbol, why should we not: (1) simply dispense with it altogether as the Quakers have done, (2) negotiate it in the interest of cross-cultural relevancy as some are willing to do (C.H. Kraft 1979:331-332), or (3) repeat it "at every crisis of religious experience" (White 1960:306)? If nothing really happens, if there is no real efficacy in Christian baptism, why not do away with it altogether, negotiate it or repeat it frequently? To these questions the "cognitive-symbolic" view of baptism (Jewett 1978:4) has no effective reply.

Therefore, I conclude that Christian baptism is not only a beautiful ritual symbol in New Testament teaching and practice but also a sacrament, an efficacious sign. As ritual symbolism Christian baptism carries a heavy load of meaning. But as sacrament Christian baptism takes us beyond mere symbolic meanings to realities. In Christian baptism as sacrament God Himself gives the benefits symbolized by the ritual.

In the chapters which follow, the reader may anticipate further evidence for these conclusions. Evidence confirming these conclusions will be presented as I answer more specifically the following questions: What was the role of baptism in the conversion of Paul? What was the role of baptism in the theology of Paul? What was the role of baptism in Paul's missionary ministry?

Notes

1. According to Charles B. Williams, "W.R. Smith (*Lectures on the Religion of the Semites*, 152-155) thinks there is a kinship between Israel's laws of uncleanness and the heathen taboo. Frazer, in *The Golden Bough*, shows numerous examples of the taboo among various tribes and nations which present striking similarity to some of Israel's laws on uncleanness."

2. Myers lists the following as scholars who favor an "older origin" of proselyte baptism: H. Mueller, R.E.O. White, H.H. Rowley, Emil Schürer, Alfred Plummer, W.O.E. Oesterley and G.H. Box, I. Abrahams, P. Billerbeck, J. Starr, H.G. Marsh, Albrecht Oepke, W.F. Flemington, Joachim Jeremias,

T.W. Manson, N. Levison, J.H. Crehan, T.F. Torrance, J. Heron, A. Gilmore, and F. Gavin (1986:9-11).

3. Cottrell quotes Zwingli's writings extensively on the topic, summarizing them as follows: "The general rule is that salvation precedes the baptism which symbolizes it" (Jack Cottrell, "Baptism According to the Reformed Tradition." In *Baptism and Remission of Sins: An Historical Perspective*, pp. 39-62). Zwingli finally came "to the position that all sacraments are symbols only" (Franklin H. Littell, *The Origins of Sectarian Protestantism*, p. 166). Hugh Thomson Kerr asserts that Zwingli "held what may be called a moral-influence theory similar to that which asserts that the sacrament has representative and symbolic value only . . . He had no tolerance of any view of the sacraments other than that they were 'bare signs'" (*The Christian Sacraments: A Source Book for Ministers*, p. 55). For further study of Zwingli's views see: Jaques Courvoisier, *Zwingli: A Reformed Theologian*, pp. 61-78 and W.P. Stephens, *The Theology of Huldrych Zwingli*, pp. 180-217. See also Cottrell, "Covenant and Baptism in the Theology of Huldreich Zwingli," an unpublished doctoral dissertation (Princeton, N.J.: Princeton Theological Seminary, 1971).

4. Scholars in the school of symbolic anthropology (SSA) ask such basic questions as: "What are the internal structures and meanings of symbolic process?" (Munn 1973:579), "What are the social co-implicates of ritual symbolism?" (V. Turner 1968:122; Munn 1973:581), and "What is the relationship between symbolic form and cultural meaning?" (Munn 1973:581). The SSA presupposes that culture is "primarily a system of symbols" (Langness 1974:117), that symbolic vehicles of ritual action are iconic (Munn 1973:605), that ritual symbolism can only be understood in the context of social process (V. Turner 1967:20), and that complex multiple meanings can be built into ritual symbolism (V. Turner 1967:284-285). Major theoretical formulations of the SSA are that: the social order is recreated through ritual activities (Munn 1973:582-583), ritual symbolism is the "switch point" between external moral constraints and internal feelings and imaginations of the individual (Munn 1973:583), ritual symbolism "fixes" social value by creating a form that celebrates it (Munn 1973:584), myth provides the link between ritual action and cultural meaning (Munn 1973:589), and ritual symbolism is instrumental toward some ends (Munn 1973:593).

5. David W. Bercot notes that Irenaeus, disciple of Polycarp who was a disciple of John the apostle, regarded John 3:5 as a reference to water baptism. Bercot quotes Irenaeus's words from *Fragments from Lost Writings*, no. 34: "As we are lepers in sin, we are made clean from our old transgressions by means of the sacred water and the invocation of the Lord. We are thus spiritually regenerated as newborn infants, even as the Lord has declared: 'Except a man be born again through water and the Spirit, he shall not enter into the kingdom of heaven'"[John 3:5] (1989:79).

6. A careful student might ask, "Is sacrament a biblical word? Why use a word not even found on the pages of Scripture to discuss the role of baptism in conversion?" My reply is that I am quite sensitive to this concern. One of the slogans of the Stone-Campbell unity movement has been "Call Bible Things by Bible Names." Yet, this slogan would rule out using "Bible" or "biblical," inasmuch as these words are not used in Scripture. The slogan would also rule out the use of the word "Christian" as an adjective since it is never so used in Scripture. Likewise, such terms as "hermeneutics," "theology," and "Trinity" are not found in Scripture. Nevertheless, such terms are helpful in discussing issues that face us as students of Scripture. In a similar way, we can use the word "sacrament" while holding a high view of the inspiration and authority of the Bible as the word of God.

7. "The Council of Trent was more exact when it declared that visible forms are sacraments only when they *represent* an invisible grace and become its channels, and when it sought further to delimit the sacramental area by reenacting (1547) a decision of the Council of Florence (1439), in which for the first time the authority of the church was given to a suggestion of Peter Lombard (12th cent.) and other schoolmen that the number of the sacraments should be fixed at seven, viz. Baptism, Confirmation, the Eucharist, Penance, Extreme Unction, Orders, and Matrimony — a suggestion which was supported by certain fanciful analogies designed to show that seven was a sacred number" (Lambert 1952:2636).

8. I concur with the Reformers and the Protestant churches in recognizing only baptism and the Lord's Supper as sacraments in this precise sense. Lambert expresses the case for this view as follows: "While, therefore, the Reformers retained the term 'sacrament' as a convenient one to express the general idea that has to be drawn from the characteristics of the rites classed together under this name, they found the distinguishing marks of sacraments (1) in their institution by Christ, (2) in their being enjoined by Him upon His followers, (3) in their being bound up with His word and revelation in such a way that they become 'the expressions of Divine thoughts, the visible symbols of Divine acts.' And as Baptism and the Lord's Supper are the only two rites for which such marks can be claimed, it follows that there are only two NT sacraments. Their unique place in the original revelation justifies us in separating them from all other rites and ceremonies that may have arisen in the history of the church, since it raises them to the dignity of forming an integral part of the historical gospel" (Lambert 1952:2637).

9. This translation of Calvin's definition of a sacrament is by Donald Bridge and David Phypers, *The Water That Divides: The Baptism Debate* (Downers Grove, IL: InterVarsity, 1977), p. 121. Bridge and Phypers then comment on Calvin's definition as follows: "'We in turn' is the crux. Just as in all of life, so in the sacraments, God takes the initiative in approaching us: we in turn then respond to him."

10. Baillie's words paraphrase Calvin who wrote as follows: "First of all, he instituted sacraments, which we who have experienced them feel to be highly useful aids to foster and strengthen faith. Shut up as we are in the prison house of our flesh, we have not yet attained angelic rank. God, therefore, in his wonderful providence accommodating himself to our capacity, has prescribed a way for us, though still far off, to draw near to him" (*Institutes*, IV, I, 1).

11. "According to the doctrine of the Rom church, sacraments are efficacious *ex opere operato*, i.e. in virtue of a power inherent in themselves as outward acts whereby they communicate saving benefits to those who receive them without opposing any obstacle. The Reformed doctrine, on the other hand, teaches that their efficacy lies not in themselves as outward acts, but in the blessing of Christ and the operation of His Spirit, and that it is conditioned by faith in the recipient. The traditional Lutheran doctrine agrees with the Reformed in affirming that faith is necessary as the condition of saving benefits in the use of the sacraments, but resembles the Rom teaching in ascribing the efficacy of Baptism and the Lord's Supper, not to the attendant working of the Holy Spirit, but to a real inherent and objective virtue resident in them — a virtue, however, which does not lie (as the Rom church says) in the mere elements and actions of the sacraments, but in the power of the Divine word which they embody" (Lambert 1952:2637).

12. Likewise, the writings of those early Christians who immediately followed the apostles are difficult to comprehend on terms other than sacramental. These Christian writers regarded baptism as more than a mere symbol. They believed that something was accomplished or effected through it. It is noteworthy, as Bercot points out, that "baptism was not an empty ritual" but that it "carried utmost significance to the early Christians" (1989:78,80). By the term "early Christians" Bercot is "primarily referring to the Christians who lived between 90 and 199 A.D." who are his main focus, but also to "writers who lived between 200 and 313, as long as their teachings agree with those who lived in the period immediately after the apostles" (1989:5-6). With regard to Jesus' words to Nicodemus, "I tell you the truth, unless a man is born of water and the Spirit, he cannot enter the kingdom of God" (John 3:5), Bercot was surprised to discover that "the early Christians *universally* understood Jesus' words to refer to water baptism" (1989:77). Bercot found (1989:79) that against the gnostics who denied this, Irenaeus (120-205) wrote: "This class of men have been instigated by Satan to a denial of that baptism which is regeneration to God" (*Heresies* bk. l, chap. 21, sec. 1). In a similar vein, he found (1989:78) that Justin Martyr (110-165) wrote, "There is no other way [to obtain God's promises] than this — to become acquainted with Christ, to be washed in the fountain spoken of by Isaiah for the remission of sins, and for the remainder, to live sinless lives" (*Trypho* chap. 44). Bercot points out (1989:79) that Clement of Alexandria (150-200) saw significant spiritual events associated with baptism: "This work is variously called grace, and illumination, and perfection, and washing. Washing, by which we cleanse away our sins. Grace, by which the penalties of our sins are canceled. And illumination, by which that holy light of salvation is beheld, that is, by which we see God clearly" (*Instructor* bk. 1, chap. 6). Bercot also notes (1989:79) that Cyprian (200-258) explained his own baptism as follows: "Considering my character at the time, I used to regard it as a difficult matter that a man should be able to be born again. . . . Or that a man who had been revived to a new life in the bath of saving water could be able to put off what he had formerly been — that he could be changed in heart and soul, while retaining his physical body. . . . I used to indulge my sins as if they were actually a part of me, inherent in me. But later, by the help of the water of new birth, the stain of former years was washed away, and a light from above — serene and pure was infused into my reconciled heart. Then through the Spirit breathed from heaven, a second birth restored me to a new man" (*To Donatus* sec. 3).

Part Two

PAULINE

PERSPECTIVES

OF BAPTISM

Chapter IV

THE ROLE OF BAPTISM IN THE CONVERSION OF PAUL

Having engaged in general background studies of both conversion and baptism, we are now in a better position to study specifically the role of baptism in Pauline theology of conversion.

In order to do this, we shall examine first the role of baptism in Paul's own conversion. Did baptism play any part at all in the actual conversion of Paul? Or was his baptism merely symbolic of a conversion which had already been culminated on the Damascus road? Why did Ananias tell Paul to be baptized (Acts 22:16)?

In order to answer these questions and to understand the role of baptism in Paul's conversion, I shall survey the Biblical narratives which refer to or describe this dramatic event. Then I shall present a detailed analysis of the role of baptism in Paul's conversion.

Paul's Conversion

The conversion of Saul of Tarsus (Acts 22:3) was one of the most important events in the life of the early church. Before his conversion, Saul gave "approval" to the death of Stephen (Acts 8:1). He breathed out "murderous threats against the Lord's disciples" (Acts 9:1). According to his own testimony, he "persecuted the church of God and tried to destroy it" (Gal 1:13). Saul "persecuted the followers" of Christ "to their death, arresting both men and women and throwing them into prison" (Acts 22:4). Finally, he traveled to Damascus with the intention of bringing Christians back to Jerusalem as prisoners (Acts 9:2; 22:5). But during this trip, he was converted to Christ (Acts 9, 22, 26). And what a conversion it was!

William Barclay calls it "the most famous conversion story in all history" (1953:71). Charles Erdman viewed Paul's conversion as one of the "strongest evidences" for the Christian faith, and asked, "how can one account for the career of Paul if he was not thus converted, and how account for his conversion if Jesus the crucified is not the divine and risen Christ?" (1949:78).

Viewing Paul's call and commission as "tightly bound together with [his] conversion" (1974:26), James Edwin Cummings described the events succinctly:

> Paul had set out on the road *to* Damascus in hopes of carrying out a mission which he thought to be according to the will of God. However, on that road, God revealed to Paul, the proud Pharisee, Jesus as the Lord exalted to heaven. Thus, on the road *from* Damascus we see a radically changed Paul (1974:15).

What happened? How did Saul, the great persecutor of the church, become Paul, the great Apostle of Christ?

The Biblical Accounts

We shall seek answers to this question, in the first place, by looking at the Biblical accounts which refer to or describe the conversion of Paul.

Although the question of which of the traditional Pauline epistles are genuine letters of Paul is a matter of scholarly debate,[1] I concur with Richard Longenecker who asserts that "there are good reasons for accepting the thirteen letters of the New Testament which claim to have been written by Paul as authentic" (1971:17). With regard to their Pauline authorship, it is significant to this study that "Romans, First and Second Corinthians, and Galatians are so strongly attested both internally and externally that few have ever questioned them" (1971:16). With regard to the conversion narratives in Acts 9, 22 and 26, I agree with Longenecker that, "there is reason for the historian to use Acts with confidence" (1971:16) and with Gilliland who affirms "that Acts is a reliable source for Pauline history" (1983:77).

Galatians 1:11-24

In Galatians Paul is "astonished" that the churches "are so quickly deserting" Christ and his gracious gospel and are "turning to a different gospel — which is really no gospel at all" (Gal 1:6-7). He views them as "foolish" and "bewitched" (Gal 3:1) inasmuch as they are trying to attain the goal by "observing the law" and "by human effort" (Gal 3:2-3). He even goes so far as to say, "You who are trying to be justified by law have been alienated from Christ; you have fallen away from grace" (Gal 5:4). Over against these legalistic tendencies, Paul reminds them of the "grace of Christ" (Gal 1:6), the "gospel of Christ" (Gal 1:7) which is what he had preached to them (Gal 1:8,11).

In defense of the gospel which he had preached and which they originally had "accepted" (Gal 1:9), Paul refers to his "previous way of life in Judaism, how intensely" he had "persecuted the church of God and tried to destroy it" (Gal 1:13). To show them that his gospel was not "from any man" but was "by revelation from Jesus Christ" (Gal 1:12), he describes the moment of God's dramatic intervention in his life:

> But when God, who set me apart from birth and called me by his grace, was pleased to reveal his Son in me so that I might preach him among the Gentiles, I did not consult any man, nor did I go up to Jerusalem to see those who

were apostles before I was, but I went immediately into
Arabia and later returned to Damascus (Gal 1:15-17).

It seems obvious that here and in the following verses Paul
"compresses all of the details of his conversion and his early
Christian life into a few phrases" (J. Cummings 1974:16).
Previously, he had been a fanatic for the law. He had been
motivated by "the rivalries and competitive spirit that animated
his training in Judaism. As a foreign Jew from Tarsus, he had to
prove equal to the best of the Palestinians" (R.T. Stamm
1953:456). Previously, in that spirit, he had been "the arch-
persecutor of the Church. He had devastated the Church. . . .
he had tried to make a scorched earth of the Church" (Barclay
1954:12). But now he is a changed man. Now he is ready to
spread that church and that gospel all over the world. Paul's
change was complete: "What he had discarded, he now picked
up; what he had hated, he now loved; what he had discounted,
he now valued; what he had scorned, he now made central;
what he had abhorred, he now adored; whom he would have
killed, he now devoted his life to serving" (O.F. Blackwelder
1953:459). How can we explain such a change? How can we
explain Paul's going full speed astern? Only by his conversion.
Barclay states it well:

> Every effect must have an adequate cause. When a man is
> proceeding headlong in one direction and suddenly turns
> and proceeds headlong in precisely the opposite direction;
> when a man suddenly reverses all his values so that his life
> turns upside down, there must be some adequate explana-
> tion. For Paul the explanation was the direct intervention of
> God (1954:12).

Paul was converted. In that conversion God took the initiative.
God was the prime mover. But Paul's response was so real and
thorough that churches of Judea heard the report: "The man
who formerly persecuted us is now preaching the faith he once
tried to destroy" (Gal 1:23). No wonder they "praised God"
(Gal 1:24) because of Paul.

1 Corinthians 9:1; 15:1-11

Paul frequently began his letters with the claim that he was "an apostle of Christ Jesus" (1 Cor 1:1; 2 Cor 1:1; Eph 1:1; Col 1:1; 1 Tim 1:1; 2 Tim 1:1; Titus 1:1). He began Galatians by writing, "Paul, an apostle — sent not from men nor by man, but by Jesus Christ and God the Father, who raised him from the dead" (Gal 1:1).

Some in the Corinthian church doubted Paul's claim to be an apostle and sat "in judgment" on him (1 Cor 9:3). His defense was to ask, "Am I not free? Am I not an apostle? Have I not seen Jesus our Lord? Are you not the result of my work in the Lord?" (1 Cor 9:1). As C.T. Craig points out, "Paul employs here the name of Jesus. It was not a mythical figure, but the Jesus of history who had appeared to him" (1953:98). On this he based his claim to be an apostle. After reminding the Corinthians of the gospel he had preached to them (1 Cor 15:1-4), Paul lists appearances of the risen Christ: "to Peter, and then to the Twelve. . . . to more than five hundred of the brothers at the same time . . . to James, then to all the apostles, and last of all he appeared to me also, as to one abnormally born" (1 Cor 15:5-8). In these references to his conversion, Paul is not giving a detailed account of all that happened. But he does stress that Christ's appearance to him was "on an equal basis with the Lord's appearances to the other disciples" (J. Cummings 1974:17).

For a more detailed description of Paul's conversion, we now turn to the accounts in Acts 9, 22, and 26. While recognizing that there are minor differences in details among these accounts, I agree with J. Cummings that they are "substantially the same" (1974:18) and with Gilliland that "there is significant unity among them" (1983:84).

Acts 9:1-19

In this account, as Saul "neared Damascus . . . a light from heaven flashed around him. He fell to the ground and heard a voice say to him, 'Saul, Saul, why do you persecute me?'" (9:3-4). He asked, "Who are you, Lord?" (9:5a). When the voice replied, "I am Jesus, whom you are persecuting, . . . Now get up and go into the city, and you will be told what you must do," Saul obeyed (9:5b-6). The men who traveled with Saul were "speechless" since "they heard the sound but did not see anyone" (9:7). When Saul "opened his eyes he could see nothing" and was led into Damascus where "for three days he was blind" and went without food and drink (9:8-9).

Then the Lord appeared in a vision to the disciple, Ananias, and told him to go to Judas's house on Straight Street where Saul was praying and expecting Ananias to come to restore his sight (9:10-12). At first, Ananias hesitated to go to such a notorious persecutor, knowing what harm he had done the church in Jerusalem and that he planned also to persecute the church in Damascus (9:13-14). Ananias overcame this understandable reluctance only when the Lord said, "Go! This man is my chosen instrument to carry my name before the Gentiles and their kings and before the people of Israel. I will show him how much he must suffer for my name" (9:15-16).

When Ananias found Saul in Judas's house, he placed his hands on him and told him that the Lord who had appeared to Saul on the road to Damascus had sent him to restore Saul's sight and that he might be "filled with the Holy Spirit" (9:17). Saul's sight was restored immediately, "he got up and was baptized," took some food and was strengthened (9:18-19).

Acts 22:1-16

In this, the second Acts account of his conversion, Paul makes his defense before the Jews in Jerusalem who were "trying to kill him" (21:31; 22:1). Addressing them in Aramaic (22:2), he reminded them of his Jewish heritage (22:3), his training under Gamaliel (22:3), his zeal for the law (22:3), and his career as a persecutor of the church, culminating in his journey for that purpose to Damascus (22:4-5).

This account is very similar to the story Luke told in Acts 9, with a few minor differences. Here Paul mentions that he saw the light "about noon" (22:6). The voice identifies himself as Jesus "of Nazareth" (22:8). Paul's companions in this account "saw the light" but "did not understand the voice" which spoke to him (22:9). Here Paul replied to the voice's self-identification as Jesus with the question, "What shall I do, Lord?" (22:10). The word "assigned" (22:10) clarifies what Paul must do and we learn that the "brilliance of the light" blinded him (22:11). There is no mention here of the Lord's appearance to Ananias to send him to Paul nor of Ananias's telling him that he would be filled with the Holy Spirit. But we learn here that Ananias was "a devout observer of the law and highly respected by all the Jews living" in Damascus (22:12). Here Ananias addresses Paul as "Brother Saul," and though there is no mention of something like scales falling from his eyes, Paul's sight is restored "at that very moment" (22:13). The message Ananias received from the Lord about Paul's future ministry (9:15-16) is here revealed to Paul by Ananias (22:14-15). Paul concludes this description of his conversion with the following command from Ananias not mentioned in the previous account: "And now what are you waiting for? Get up, be baptized and wash your sins away, calling on his name" (22:16). There is no mention here of Paul's breaking his fast.

Acts 26:1-18

The third Acts account of Paul's conversion is given by Paul as he defends himself before King Agrippa whom he regards as knowledgeable of Jewish customs and controversies (26:1-3). He again refers to his Jewish heritage, stresses his life as a Pharisee, and regards himself as on trial because of the fulfillment of God's promises to Israel, even though some might consider the resurrection incredible (26:4-8). He reviews his career as a persecutor of the church, mentioning here that he "put many of the saints in prison," cast his "vote against them" when "they were put to death," and that he persecuted them from synagogue to synagogue and even in "foreign cities" trying to "force them to blaspheme" (26:9-11).

In this account, although Paul and his companions all fell to the ground, there is no mention of Paul's blindness. The voice spoke to him in "Aramaic" and the words, "It is hard for you to kick against the goads" are added (26:12-14).[2] Here the words about Paul's ministry which Ananias received in a vision (9:15-16) and which he communicated to Paul (22:14-15) are presented as spoken directly to Paul by Jesus (26:16-18). There is no mention here of Ananias or of Paul's three days of fasting nor of his baptism.

There are minor differences in details among these narratives. However, I concur with Longenecker that the differences or problems are of the "type frequently found in a comparison of the Synoptic Gospels — and, for that matter, found in any correlation of two or more separate narratives of any one historical event" (1971:32).[3] Paul's conversion was real, and the attention Luke gave it in three extended narratives indicates the importance he attached to it.

Paul's Conversion: Its Reality and Significance

With regard to the reality of Jesus' appearance to Paul as the basis for his conversion, Ladd states it squarely:

> The only real alternatives for interpreting Paul's conversion are agnosticism — which is no solution — or the actual appearance of Jesus Christ to his senses on the way to Damascus, which is Paul's own interpretation. Nothing but his certainty of the reality of Jesus' appearance could have convinced him that Jesus was raised from the dead, and was therefore the Messiah and the Son of God. Nothing but the fact itself can, under the circumstances, fairly account for his certainty (1974:368).

Johannes Weiss expresses it this way:

> The special point in the Damascus experience was that he
> became convinced from that time on that the heavenly
> Messiah was none other than the crucified Jesus. The
> appearance which he saw must not only have borne the
> marks of the glorified Messiah, it must also in some way or
> other have contained features by which he recognized Jesus.
> . . . But, whatever antecedents the event may have had, it
> cannot be doubted that the vital point in it was Paul's con-
> victions of *the identity of the heavenly Messiah with the cruci-
> fied Jesus* (1937:191).

Moreover, Paul's conversion is of great significance in the
present day since it affords one of the strongest evidences of
the truth of the Christian faith: for "how can we account for
the career of Paul if he was not thus converted, and how account
for his conversion if Jesus the crucified is not the divine and
risen Christ" (Erdman 1949:78). J. Gresham Machen expressed
the same idea in this language:

> The religion of Paul is a fact which stands in the full light of
> history. How is it to be explained? What were its presuppo-
> sitions? Upon what sort of Jesus was it founded? . . .
> Explain the origin of the religion of Paul, and you have
> solved the problem of the origin of Christianity (1947:4-5).

Then, after more than three hundred pages of study Machen
concluded:

> The religion of Paul was not founded upon a complex
> of ideas derived from Judaism or from paganism. It was
> founded upon the historical Jesus. But the historical Jesus
> upon whom it was founded was not the Jesus of modern
> reconstruction, but the Jesus of the whole New Testament
> and of Christian faith; not a teacher who survived only in
> the memory of His disciples, but the Saviour who after His
> redeeming work was done still lived and could be loved
> (1947:317).

Paul's conversion was real, and it was one of the most important events in the life of the early church. What a conversion! "At once he began to preach in the synagogues that Jesus is the Son of God" (Acts 9:20). The Jews in both Damascus (Acts 9:23) and in Jerusalem (Acts 9:29) tried to kill him. But "the church throughout Judea, Galilee and Samaria enjoyed a time of peace" (Acts 9:31). Then Paul began a life of almost unbelievable service, suffering, and sacrifice in the name of Him whom he once persecuted (1 Cor 15:9-10; 2 Cor 11:24-28). Who could measure his influence as an apostle, as a planter of churches, or as an author of many of the books of the New Testament? Paul was a man of great stature as a missionary, founder of churches, and a hero of the faith. Therefore, who could measure the influence of his conversion?

But what part did *baptism* play in Paul's conversion? Was Paul's conversion complete on the Damascus road, or was it complete when Ananias baptized him? Let us now examine the evidence in these narratives to answer this crucial question.

An Analysis of the Role of Baptism in Paul's Conversion

Paul's conversion was a part of a process. It did not happen in a void. His whole childhood and early training; his relationship with Gamaliel; his relationship to the Sadducean Sanhedrin; his response to Hellenism and the death of Stephen; and, finally, the Damascus road experience: all these events and others were preparatory to or involved in Paul's conversion. Like all other conversions, Paul's conversion was a process which took place within a context, not a vacuum (Gilliland 1983:77-84).

But the question we shall examine here is the question of whether *baptism* was a part of that process. Was Paul's conversion complete on the Damascus road, or was it culminated when Ananias baptized him? What was the role or function of baptism in his conversion? Obviously, repentance and faith were crucial aspects of his conversion even though neither is mentioned in the Biblical accounts.

Surprisingly, the conversion narratives themselves contain no record of Paul's being *commanded* either to believe or to repent. As a matter of fact, neither the word "faith" nor the word "repentance" is ever mentioned, not even once, with reference to Paul in any of the three narratives of his conversion to Christ (Acts 9:1-19; 22:1-16; 26:1-18).

Nevertheless, there is no doubt that Paul repented. These narratives describe the time in this man's life when he went "full speed astern." He experienced that change of mind which is produced by godly sorrow and results in a changed life (2 Cor 7:10). Paul, during his conversion, underwent the change described in the New Testament by the Greek words ἐπιστρέφω (*epistrepho*) and μετανοέω (*metanoeo*). Paul repented.

Moreover, during his conversion Paul also came to believe on Christ as Risen Lord and Savior. When Paul was baptized, he confessed his faith in Christ by "calling on his name" (Acts 22:16). He trusted Christ, not self, for salvation (Phil 3:4-14). He who once persecuted Christ now proclaimed him as the Son of God (Acts 9:20). From this point on, he regarded the gospel of Christ as the power of God unto salvation (Rom 1:16) and was willing to spend all his remaining years proclaiming it. Hence, repentance and faith were very important in Paul's conversion, as they are in all real conversions to Christ.

The Acts Narratives

But what do the Acts narratives say of Paul's *baptism?* What was the place of baptism in the conversion of Paul? What do the narratives themselves actually say?

Baptism Was Something Paul Was Told He "Must Do" (Acts 9:3-6; 22:10-11,16)

After Saul saw the light on the Damascus road, he heard a

voice which said to him, "'Saul, Saul, why do you persecute me?' 'Who are you, Lord?' Saul asked. 'I am Jesus, whom you are persecuting,' he replied. 'Now get up and go into the city, and you will be told what you *must* do'" (Acts 9:3-6; emphasis mine). When Ananias came to him, he said to him, among other things, "Get up, be baptized and wash your sins away, calling on his name" (Acts 22:16). When Saul heard Ananias telling him to be baptized, he heard him telling him something that he *must* do. Moreover, the Greek verb form used here, βάπτισαι (*baptisai*, "be baptized") is an imperative, a form which implies a command. Hence, in these conversion narratives, Paul was told that he must be baptized. A careful reading of the records does not leave one with the impression that baptism was an optional matter.

Baptism Was Something Paul Actually Did (Acts 9:9,11,18)

As a matter of fact, Paul actually was baptized, as were the other believers whose cases of conversion are given to us as models in the extended conversion narratives in Acts (Acts 2:22-40; 8:26-39; 10:1-48; 16:13-15; 16:16-34; 18:1-8).

In this connection, one might wonder, if Paul's conversion was consummated, his sins forgiven, his soul at peace with God at some point before baptism, why he continued in prayer and fasting until he was baptized. If Paul's conversion was culminated on the Damascus road, why did a period of prayer and fasting, rather than rejoicing, immediately follow?

In a similar vein, Beasley-Murray sees Paul's baptism not only as something he actually did but also as something he actually did as a part of his conversion. He sees it as "axiomatic that conversion and baptism are inseparable" and asserts that in the "primitive apostolic church baptism was 'conversion baptism.'" Beasley-Murray discusses the role of baptism in some of the Acts conversion narratives, including Paul's, as follows:

The converts of the great Pentecost, looking back on that momentous day, would never have distinguished between their response of faith and their baptism as two separable events. Their baptism was their response. The same applies to the Philippian Jailer, and despite the uniqueness attaching to the conversion of Paul and of the household of Cornelius, the same principle holds good for them. For although the Lord had dealt catastrophically and decisively with Saul in his meeting on the Damascus road, he remained in blindness till the coming of Ananias, and not till after his baptism did he take food and resume normal life. *For Paul his baptism completed his conversion* (Acts ix.19). It would have done no less for Cornelius and his friends (Acts x.47 ff.), in spite of the exceptional nature of their experience (1966:37-38; emphasis mine).

Notice, too, that Paul would have been quite aware of such antecedents of Christian baptism as Old Testament lustrations, Jewish proselyte baptism, Qumran baptisms, and the baptism of John. He would also have been quite aware of the meaning of baptism as practiced by those who followed Jesus as their Crucified-Risen Messiah. Moreover, Paul knew, if anyone did, how dangerous it might be for him to be baptized. But he obeyed the command, nevertheless, and then faced the consequences. In these conversion narratives, Paul actually was baptized.

Baptism Was Something Paul Did in Addition to Fasting and Praying (Acts 9:9,11)

After he saw Christ and was blinded on the road to Damascus, Saul was blind for three days during which he "did not eat or drink anything" (Acts 9:9). The Lord instructed Ananias to "go to the house of Judas on Straight Street and ask for a man from Tarsus named Saul, *for he is praying*" (Acts 9:11; emphasis mine). Why did Saul fast and pray for three days instead of rejoicing? No doubt he wanted to see again. It is very likely that he prayed for the restoration of his sight. Possibly, he prayed for fuller understanding of what had happened to him, of what he had seen and heard on the Damascus road. One can imagine many praises and petitions Saul might have offered up to the Lord. But who can doubt that he wanted forgiveness? By persecuting the church of the Christ he had persecuted the Christ of the church (Acts 9:5). Who can doubt that, blind as he was physically, Saul could see, even then, that Christ had come "into the world to save sinners — of whom" he, Saul, was "the worst"? (1 Tim 1:15). Surely, he was praying what is often called, "The Sinner's Prayer." Surely, he was asking the Lord Jesus to forgive him, to take his sins away. Surely, he expressed verbally his repentance and faith. But that was not enough. The "Sinner's Prayer" was not enough! Ananias told him to do something more than pray. Instead, he told him to be baptized (Acts 22:16). It appears that being told to pray the "Sinner's Prayer" is a modern functional substitute for baptism!

Baptism Was Something Ananias Told Him to Do (Acts 22:16)

After the Lord helped Ananias to overcome his understandable reluctance to go to Saul, he found him in the house where he was staying, told him that God had chosen him to be a "witness to all men of what [he had] seen and heard" (Acts 22:14-15), and then he asked him, "What are you waiting for? Get up, be baptized and wash your sins away, calling on his name" (Acts 22:16). As pointed out by J.W. McGarvey, "a human messenger is made to tell the sinner what to do, even after the Lord himself has appeared to him, and the human messenger helps him to do what he is told to do by baptizing him" (1892:179). This human messenger, Ananias, was a "disciple" (Acts 9:10) who knew of the harm Saul had done to the Lord's "saints in Jerusalem" (Acts 9:13) and that he was in Damascus with "authority from the chief priests to arrest" the disciples of Christ there (Acts 9:14). When Ananias baptized Saul, he did so as a disciple of Christ, as a member of Christ's body, the church, which Saul had persecuted. That Saul was incorporated into the church when Ananias baptized him is indicated by Saul's spending "several days with the disciples in Damascus" (Acts 9:19) immediately after his baptism. Whatever else baptism was in Paul's conversion, it was something that Ananias commanded him to do.

Baptism Was Something Connected with Washing Away His Sins (Acts 22:16)

It would seem that only a person with little or no knowledge of Biblical teaching about baptism would understand this to mean that there was a magical power in the water or in the isolated act of baptism that could wash away sins. There is no basis here upon which to build a doctrine of "baptismal regeneration." Nevertheless, baptism and the washing away of sins are closely connected in Ananias's injunction to the penitent believer, Saul. What was the connection?

Ananias urged Saul, "And now what are you waiting for? Get up, be baptized and wash your sins away, calling on his name" (Acts 22:16). Cottrell points out: "Ananias's instruction to Saul includes two aorist participles, 'rising up' and 'calling upon'; and two imperatives, 'be baptized' and 'wash away your sins.' This last item is the crucial one. What does it mean to 'wash away' sins?" (1989:71).

To answer his question Cottrell stresses the "close connection" here "between baptism and the washing away of sins" and affirms that "the most natural understanding is that the former is somehow the occasion or the condition of the latter" (1989:71-72). As Cottrell sees it, this is true for several reasons. First, since Saul was under "deep conviction of his sins," he would "most naturally take baptism to be what he should do to wash his sins away" (1989:72). Second, Cottrell says:

> This view is consistent with other New Testament teaching about baptism and salvation in general and with its teaching about baptism and forgiveness in particular. It is in effect

the exact equivalent of Peter's instruction in Acts 2:38. "Be baptized for the forgiveness of your sins" means the very same thing as "be baptized and wash away your sins" (1989:72).

Third, according to Cottrell, "the very fact that Saul is instructed with an *imperative* to *wash away his sins* shows that it must be the result of baptism" (1989:72). Cottrell notes that the washing away of sins is ultimately a divine act through the blood of Christ and not the act of any human being. No mere human being can wash away his sins. Yet, Saul is commanded to do so. How does this make sense? How could Saul wash away his sins? Cottrell answers that this is impossible "*unless* the washing away of sins was dependent on something he *could* do, namely, submit to Christian baptism. This is the implication of the fact that 'wash away' is in the imperative form" (1989:72). Cottrell continues:

> Finally, the *number* and *order* of the imperatives show that baptism is a condition for washing away sins. If the outward act were *only* a symbolic picture of a prior inner cleansing, we would not expect him to put both in the imperative form. In such a case it would be appropriate for the "washing away" to be an aorist participle (like "rising up" and "calling upon"). Strictly speaking the action of an aorist participle *precedes* the action of the main verb. Ananias thus would have said, "Be baptized [imperative], having washed away your sins [aorist participle]." But he does not say this; he uses two imperatives instead (1989:72-73).

Still, does the mere use of the two imperatives mean that baptism is for the washing away of sins? No, not if the order of the verbs were different. If the order had been reversed to say, "Wash away your sins and be baptized," baptism could be regarded as simply symbolic of a prior cleansing. But, as it is, "be baptized" precedes "wash away your sins." Hence, Cottrell comments: "This order of the two imperatives, along with the other reasons cited above, requires us to conclude that baptism is a preceding condition for the washing away or forgiveness of sins" (1989:73).

Baptism Was Something to Be Done Calling on the Name of the Lord (Acts 22:16)

Whatever was to be the benefit of baptism for Paul was to accrue to him with reference to "calling on the name of the Lord." Doubtless this reminded Paul of the Old Testament promise, "everyone who calls on the name of the LORD will be saved" (Joel 2:32), which he later quoted in the most "theological" of his books (Rom 10:13). Apparently, baptism was something which, like faith and repentance, had a value only as it related to Christ and calling upon His name. Neither faith, repentance, nor baptism had a magical or meritorious value or a value or benefit *per se* in isolation from calling on the name of Christ and Him whom that name represents.

It is crucial here, as Cottrell points out (1989:75), to ask "*for what purpose* or *to what end* was Saul told to call upon the name of the Lord?*" The answer seems quite clear, for as Cottrell expressed it,

> He must call upon the name of the Lord *for salvation*. This is Joel's point: "Whoever calls on the name of the LORD *will be delivered*." This is how Peter and Paul quote it: whoever calls on the name of the Lord *will be saved*. Paul equates it with the confession of the mouth that Jesus is Lord, a confession that results in salvation (Rom. 10:9-10; cf. 10:13).

Cottrell goes on to say:

> As it applied to Saul it meant two things. First, the fact that he was supposed to call upon the Lord's name in connection with his baptism meant that he had not yet received salvation. The whole point of his calling upon the Lord's name was *to be saved*. Thus this is one final confirmation of the conclusion already reached above, that Saul was not saved on the Damascus Road nor during his three days of fasting and prayer. He was not saved until he called upon

the Lord's name in baptism. Second, this "calling upon His name" was an indication of Saul's *faith* in Jesus (1989:75-76).

Thus, by his baptism as an integral part of his total conversion experience, Paul was calling on the name of the Lord for salvation.

Baptism Was Something to Be Done without "Waiting" (Acts 22:16)

Being baptized without waiting accords with other cases of conversion in Acts. On Pentecost day, "those who accepted his message were baptized, and about three thousand were added to their number *that day*" (Acts 2:41; emphasis mine). Philip baptized the Ethiopian eunuch after one lesson based on Isaiah 53.

> Then Philip began with that very passage of Scripture and told him the good news about Jesus.
> As they traveled along the road, they came to some water and the eunuch said, "Look, here is water. Why shouldn't I be baptized?" And he gave orders to stop the chariot. Then both Philip and the eunuch went down into the water and Philip baptized him (Acts 8:35-38).

Cornelius and his household also were baptized after hearing just one sermon (Acts 10:47-48). The Philippian jailer and his house responded after only one sermon from Paul and Silas.

> At that hour of the night the jailer took them and washed their wounds; then immediately he and all his family were baptized. The jailer brought them into his house and set a meal before them; and he was filled with joy, because he had come to believe in God — he and his whole family (Acts 16:33-34).

As in so many other cases, baptism was, in Paul's case, something which was to be done without waiting. There was an urgency in the words of Ananias concerning Paul's baptism.

Paul's Baptism According to Paul

The only *Pauline* explanation we have of the place of baptism in his conversion is found in his own words in Romans 6:3-4:

> Or don't you know that all of us who were baptized into Christ Jesus were baptized into his death? We were therefore buried with him through baptism into death in order that, just as Christ was raised from the dead through the glory of the Father, we too may live a new life.

By using the phrase, "all of us who were baptized into Christ Jesus," Paul includes himself as well as the Romans among those who had been baptized. He also states that both he and they "were baptized into Christ Jesus" and that both he and they "were baptized into his death" (Rom 6:3). We will engage in a more detailed study of these verses a little later. However, at this point it is clear that Paul regarded baptism as the occasion during which he and the Romans were incorporated into Christ and when they became somehow connected with his death.

Summary

To summarize this study of the role or function of baptism in the conversion of Paul, it is evident that baptism was an integral part of the total process of his conversion. It was what Ananias told Paul he must do. It was a commanded action which had some connection with the washing away of Paul's sins. Paul actually was baptized calling on the name of the Lord. Indeed, it is clear from these narratives that baptism was such an urgent and important matter that we can regard it as a part of Paul's conversion rather than being merely symbolic of a conversion which was concluded without it on the Damascus road. It was not merely a part of the aftermath of Paul's conversion but a part of the conversion event which was consummated by it.

Is it not clear, then, that the Damascus road experience was Paul's encounter with the Risen Lord? It was this dramatic encounter which caused Saul, the "arch-persecutor" of Christ and His church, to believe. Because of this unexpected confrontation, he suddenly saw himself as guilty of blasphemy and of persecuting the church and Christ Himself. He repented. Although neither faith nor repentance are mentioned in the Acts narratives which relate the conversion of Paul, who can doubt that he trusted Christ and that he truly repented of his sins? Who can doubt that, during three days of prayer and fasting in Damascus, Paul was asking the Lord Jesus to forgive him, to take his sins away? He was praying the "Sinner's Prayer." But that was not enough. He was told to do more. He was told to do something that would express his faith and repentance, something that would complete his conversion. Ananias told him, "And now what are you waiting for? Get up, be baptized and wash your sins away, calling on his name" (Acts 22:16). When the penitent believer, Saul of Tarsus, obeyed this command, the command to be baptized, his conversion was culminated.

The idea that Paul's baptism had no connection with his conversion apart from a symbolic function misses the deep meaning of baptism. In baptism, Paul received the washing of forgiveness, and he was incorporated into Christ's body. In baptism his conversion was consummated.

Notes

1. For a defense of the Pauline authorship of the epistles traditionally ascribed to him see: Donald Guthrie, *New Testament Introduction, The Pauline Epistles* (Chicago: InterVarsity, 1961) and Everett Harrison, *Introduction to the New Testament* (Grand Rapids: Eerdmans, 1964).

2. According to F.J. Foakes-Jackson and Kirsopp Lake, the saying, "It is hard for you to kick against the goads," is found "in the B-text only in this passage, but it is inserted in ix.5 in the African Latin and the Harclean margin, and in the Harclean margin in xxii 7; D is not extant in ix.5, but does not have the addition in xxii.7." After citing various Greek and Latin writers who used this proverb, the authors assert that it "has not yet been found in any Aramaic source" but "appears to be, like the use of the LXX in Peter's

speeches, an indication that the speeches in Acts are the composition of the editor, not translations from the Aramaic, even when, as here, the speaker is said to have been using that language." As to its meaning, we are informed that "the proverb is used in poetry particularly of resisting fate or the will of the gods" and that "The goad, called in the A.V. 'prick,' is usually mentioned in the singular (though here it is plural) and is a sharp-pointed stick. It is known to the Old Testament writers as used to prod an ox or ass at the plough (or horse, Ps.Sol. xvi.4). The word 'hard' . . . does not mean 'difficult' but indicates that it hurts the one who resists or kicks" (F.J. Foakes-Jackson and Kirsopp Lake, *The Acts of the Apostles, Volume IV: English Translation and Commentary* [Grand Rapids: Baker, 1979], pp. 318-319).

3. For a discussion of differences among the Acts accounts of Paul's conversion see: Richard Longenecker, *The Ministry and Message of Paul* (Grand Rapids: Zondervan, 1971).

Chapter V

THE ROLE OF BAPTISM IN PAULINE THEOLOGY

Having engaged in general background studies of both conversion and baptism, and having examined the role of baptism in Paul's own conversion, we are now prepared to study the role of baptism in Pauline theology.

Beasley-Murray found baptism in sixteen passages in the writings of Paul (1962:vii,viii). However, it is disputed whether Colossians 1:13f, 2:15; 1 Corinthians 6:11; 2 Corinthians 1:22; Ephesians 1:13, 4:30; 1 Corinthians 7:14; Ephesians 5:25-27; 1 Timothy 6:12-13; 2 Timothy 2:11-12; or Titus 3:5-7, although found on Beasley-Murray's list, actually refer to baptism. Hence, such passages will not be studied here. Nor will I attempt to explain such difficult passages as 1 Corinthians 15:29 or 1 Corinthians 10:1f; for, whatever their true meaning is, baptism "for the dead" and baptism "into Moses" do not refer to the role of baptism in conversion. I am also passing over these verses on the principle that "it is preferable to interpret obscure passages in the light of the clear than to proceed vice versa" (Beasley-Murray 1962:126).

Even the remaining passages (Romans 6:1-4; Galatians 3:26-27; Colossians 2:11-14; 1 Corinthians 12:13; 1 Corinthians 1:11-17; and Ephesians 4:5) are too numerous to study in this chapter. Instead, I shall examine only Romans 6:1-4; Galatians

3:26-27; and Colossians 2:11-14, passages which Beasley-Murray regards as "cardinal" or "characteristic" Pauline passages on baptism (1962:126). Moreover, since even these passages discuss many topics other than the role of baptism in conversion, I will not attempt a detailed exegesis of them. Rather, I will examine them to discover what light they cast on the role of baptism in conversion. These three passages will be studied with the conviction that Paul's understanding of baptism here is consistent with its place in his own conversion and ministry, as well as in harmony with his total theology.

United with Christ

> What shall we say, then? Shall we go on sinning so that grace may increase? By no means! We died to sin; how can we live in it any longer? Or don't you know that all of us who were baptized into Christ Jesus were baptized into his death? We were therefore buried with him through baptism into death in order that, just as Christ was raised from the dead through the glory of the Father, we too may live a new life (Rom 6:1-4).

Context

These verses were not written primarily to discuss or explain baptism. Rather, Paul is here answering a possible objection to the doctrine of salvation by grace. A few verses earlier he had written, "where sin increased, grace increased all the more" (Rom 5:20). Paul had taught that human sin had occasioned the gift of divine grace to fallen humanity. God's grace was extended through Christ crucified in order to free sinners from death and to enable them to live the new life free from the power of sin. But, contrary to this, some might conclude that "to go on sinning" was the proper response to God's grace. Paul rejects this idea. He replies, "By no means!" (Rom 6:2). His chief argument against such possible cheapening of divine grace is that, through Christ, we have been set free from sin, we have been baptized!

As Beasley-Murray points out, Paul could have answered the heresy, "Let us go on sinning so that grace may increase," with a purely theoretical consideration: "'Under no circumstances! Such conduct would frustrate the intention of grace.' Instead he appealed to an event in the past on which it would be unthinkable to go back: 'We died to sin once; how can we live in it still?'" (1962:143). It is in fuller explanation of the idea that it is "unthinkable" for the Roman Christians to "go on sinning" that Paul discusses baptism. When Paul wants to lead these early believers away from cheap grace, he says, "Remember your baptism! The baptized have died to sin. How can you, the baptized, still live in what you have died to?"

Union with Christ

A fundamental concept in Romans 6:1-4 is that the Roman Christians had been "baptized into Christ Jesus," into a saving union with Him who had died for them.

Cottrell reminds us that "the concept of union with Christ occurs quite frequently in Scripture." He regards union with Christ as a "comprehensive description of the saved state" and goes on to say: "All other aspects of salvation come to us as the result of our being united with Christ" (1989:80). He depicts Scriptural teaching about the believer's union with Christ as follows:

> The terminology expressing this union varies, but the main terms are that we are in Christ and Christ is in us. Regarding the former, for example, Paul refers to "all the saints *in Christ Jesus*" at Philippi (Phil. 1:1; See Col. 1:2); and Peter declares, "Peace be to you all who are *in Christ*" (I Pet. 5:14). "By His doing you are *in Christ Jesus*," says Paul (I Cor. 1:30). Regarding the other expression, Paul says that as Christians you should know "that Jesus Christ is *in you*" (II Cor. 13:5). "If Christ is *in you*," he says, your spirit

is alive (Rom. 8:10). "Christ *in you*" is "the hope of glory" (Col. 1:27). Thus he prays "that Christ may *dwell in your hearts*" (Eph. 3:17). "It is no longer I who live, but Christ *lives in me*," is his testimony of himself (Gal. 2:20) (1989:80).

For us to be in Christ and for Christ to be in us refers not to a physical union but to a relationship with Christ which is "so close that all the power and life that spring from His redeeming work belong to us and flow into our lives. All the redemptive benefits of His death, burial, and resurrection are ours" (1989:81).

John Murray sees the fact of the believer's having died to sin as the "fundamental premise" in Romans 6:1-4 and asserts that "the tense used in this instance is one that points to a definite act in the past." That "definite act in the past," according to Murray, is baptism which "signifies union with Christ in his death." Affirming that Paul's readers were "aware of the place and importance of baptism in the Christian profession," Murray discusses what it means to be baptized into union with Christ:

> Baptism "into Jesus Christ" means baptism into union with Christ. To be baptized "into Moses" (I Cor. 10:2) is to be baptized into the discipleship of Moses or into the participation of the privileges which the Mosaic economy entailed. . . . To be baptized "into the name of the Father and of the Son and of the Holy Ghost" (Matt. 28:19) is to be baptized into the fellowship of the three persons of the Godhead. Hence baptism into Christ signifies simply union with him and participation of all the privileges which he as Christ Jesus embodies (1959:214).

What are the "redemptive benefits" or the "privileges" into which a believer enters when entering into union with Christ? Merely to list such benefits or privileges is impressive. According to Scripture the spiritual benefits found "in Christ" are as follows: no condemnation (Rom 8:1), forgiveness (Eph 1:7; Col

1:14), new creaturehood (2 Cor 5:17), redemption (Eph 1:7; Col 1:14) and salvation (2 Tim 2:10). Perhaps most impressive and comprehensive of all is Paul's sweeping assertion that "every spiritual blessing" is "in Christ" (Eph 1:3). Hence, baptism "into Christ Jesus" is baptism into all the "spiritual benefits" or "privileges" listed above. Baptism "into Christ Jesus" is baptism into no condemnation, forgiveness, new creaturehood, redemption, salvation and all spiritual blessings. The list is indeed impressive. So also is that union by which believers enter into Christ Jesus and in which they participate when they are baptized!

Incorporation into Christ

This union may also be seen as an incorporation, a uniting so as to form one body. Anders Nygren asserts that the reason for the discussion in Romans 6 was the question, "Are we to continue in sin that grace may abound?" He continues, "The strongest answer with which he could meet that question was precisely by referring to baptism and what happens through it" (1949:239). But what is this? What happens through baptism? A few pages earlier Nygren wrote, "But now, through baptism, we have been incorporated into Christ. That means that we are henceforth not merely members in the great organism of humanity; we are members in "the body of Christ" . . . "By *one* Spirit we were all baptized into *one* body" (1949:233).

When Paul wrote, "For we were all baptized by one Spirit into one body" (1 Cor 12:13), he made explicit a concept which was implicit in his saying we were "baptized into Christ Jesus" (Rom 6:3). The connection between Christ and the body of Christ is such that to be baptized into one is to be baptized into the other. One could not be in the body of Christ without being in Christ Himself. One could not be in Christ without being in His body. The body of Christ is the church of Christ (Eph 1:22-23; 3:6; 4:4; Col 1:18,24).

Paul's thought here, however, is not merely the concept of a local congregation or fellowship. Instead, he is thinking of the one universal body (Eph 4:4) which believers enter at baptism. As Cottrell points out, "the New Testament *never* depicts baptism as simply a public act by which one enters some visible, local congregation. It is always a matter of . . . entry into the invisible, universal church that is the body of Christ" (1989: 99). To be baptized into Christ, into his spiritual body, the church, is, as Harold M. Daniels observed, to be baptized into a "big family":

> While baptism takes place in a particular congregation, it marks one's entrance into the body of Christ that transcends every division resulting from human failure and pride. . . . While the names of the newly baptized are recorded on the membership roll of a particular community of the baptized, in their baptism they are joined to the company of the faithful that transcends sect or tradition. . . . The baptized have many brothers and sisters. It is a big family. . . . My brothers and sisters are all those from every time and place who have been washed in the waters of baptism (1995:88).

Whoever, therefore, is baptized into Christ is also at that time baptized into the body or church of Christ, whatever local church he or she may join at that time or later. In this same vein, Nygren comments as follows:

> Through baptism we have been received into the new age, which began in the resurrection of Christ. He who has been baptized into Christ has been incorporated into Him; he is "in Christ." II Corinthians 5:17 is the best conceivable commentary on the point under discussion. "If anyone is in Christ, he is a new creation; the old has passed away, behold, the new has come." He who, through baptism, is in Christ is a new creation, a new man, formed according to the nature of the new aeon (1949:235).

William Sanday also sees baptism as "an act of *incorporation* into Christ." According to Sanday, "This conception lies at the root of the whole passage. All the consequences which St. Paul draws follow from this union, incorporation, identification . . . with Christ" (1895:156).

Hence, our union with Christ through baptism, our incorporation into Christ through baptism into His death is a fundamental concept in this passage. According to Cottrell, our benefits through union with Christ are no less than what he calls a "double cure." As Cottrell sees it, the "double cure" is made possible by the death of Christ:

> Since Jesus died for the express purpose of taking our guilt upon Himself and paying the eternal penalty for our sins, when we are united with Him in his death our guilt is removed and our status before God is such that our penalty is considered paid. . . .
>
> But there is more. Our union with Christ also provides us with the other part of the double cure, namely, our regeneration or rebirth to new life. . . . Being united with Christ in *His* death, burial, and resurrection means that we experience a death, burial, and resurrection of our own. Just as Christ died with reference to the sins of the whole world, in our union with Him we die to our own sin (Rom. 6:10-11). Our old sin-prone self actually experiences a death (Rom. 6:6) and is buried out of sight just as Jesus was (Rom. 6:4). Then, just as Jesus arose from the dead, in our union with Him we too experience an actual resurrection from spiritual death and begin to live a new life (1989:81).

Thus through union with Christ we are saved from both the guilt and power of sin. If so, as Cottrell affirms, "We can see, then, how crucially important our union with Christ is. It is the key to our salvation" (1989:82).

When Does Union with Christ Occur?

But when does this union with Christ occur? When does the new convert, the person who is turning initially to Christ in faith and repentance, enter into union with Christ and receive the spiritual benefits and privileges which are in Him?

Romans 6:1-4 is quite clear on this point. The Roman Christians had entered into union with Christ when they were baptized into Him, baptized into His death and resurrection. When they were baptized, the Roman believers had entered into a relationship with Christ from which they received all the redemptive benefits and spiritual blessings which are "in Christ." It was when they were baptized that these early believers entered into union with Christ, a union in which they received forgiveness, redemption, salvation, new creaturehood and all other spiritual blessings.

According to Cottrell, "Romans 6:3-4 affirms that *baptism* is the time when we are united with Christ in His death and resurrection, and thus the time when we experience our own death to sin and resurrection to new life" (1989:83). Flemington describes baptism as a "re-enactment for the believer of what once happened to our Lord" (1948:59). Beasley-Murray translates H. Schlier's comment on this as follows: "The same thing has happened to Christ and to us; *as* it happened to Him, *so* it has happened to us. When? As we became baptized to Christ" (1962:131). The believer's union with Christ, as presented in this passage, occurs at the time of the believer's own baptism.[1]

However, this understanding differs from the "cognitive-symbolic" view of baptism (Jewett 1978:4) which holds that sinners enter into saving union with Christ when they first believe, or when they first believe, repent, and "receive Christ into their hearts." Although the exact formulation differs from church to church and from evangelist to evangelist, what various expressions of this view have in common is the concept that saving union with Christ occurs at some time *before* baptism. According to this view, the sinner's death to sin and resurrection to new life in Christ takes place at the time when the sinner's heart turns to God in initial saving faith and repentance.

However, if this view is correct, if new converts enter into saving union with Christ at the point of their initial saving faith and repentance, the sense of urgency about baptism in Paul's own conversion (or in any other new believer's conversion) is greatly diminished. If baptism merely symbolizes a saving union with Christ which took place at some time prior to the new convert's baptism, there would be little sense of urgency about it. If baptism merely symbolizes a saving union with Christ which has already occurred prior to baptism and without it, then baptism could be delayed for further instructions, for acceptance of a church's creedal statement, for ecclesiastical examination of a candidate's motives, or for inclement weather. In fact, if new converts come into saving union with Christ when their hearts first turn to God in cognitive faith and/or repentance, baptism could be delayed for whatever reason any church or individual thought best. And, as I pointed out earlier, if baptism is a mere symbol of salvation which the convert has already received, why not dispense with it altogether or negotiate it for some other form in the interest of cross-cultural relevancy? The "cognitive-symbolic" view of baptism has no valid answers to these questions.

Moreover, the view that new converts enter into saving union with Christ at the point of initial cognitive faith and/or repentance, prior to the expression of faith and repentance in baptism, is contrary to the clear teaching of the passage that the Roman Christians were "baptized into Christ Jesus," that they were "baptized into his death," and that they were "buried with him through baptism into death."

The word "into" translates the Greek word εἰς (*eis*) which we will discuss in greater depth when we study Galatians 3:26-27. Suffice it to say here, however, that the basic meaning of *eis* indicates motion toward or entrance into something, including the concepts of goal or purpose (Arndt and Gingrich 1979: 228-230). Other meanings of *eis* are possible. But the causal meaning "because of" is controversial as indicated in the following entry in Arndt and Gingrich (1979:230).

Other uses of *eis*—**a.** *at, in the face of . . . repent at the proclamation* Mt 12:41; Lk 11:32; cf. Ro. 4:20 and perh.

Mt 3:11. JRMantey . . . argues for a causal use here *because of the proclam.* . . ; against him RMarcus . . .

There is no doubt that *eis* may be translated with a meaning similar to that of ἐν (*en*), in which the meaning would be "with respect to" or "with reference to." But such a meaning is relatively infrequent (Arndt and Gingrich 1979:230). Hence, unless the context gives strong support for the controversial meaning "because of" or the infrequent meaning "with reference to," it is best to translate *eis* with such forward looking words as "into," "unto," or "toward." This is, of course, what our translators have done in Romans 6:1-4.

But, as mentioned before, the view that new converts enter into a saving union with Christ prior to baptism is contrary to the teaching that these early converts were "baptized into Christ Jesus," "baptized into his death," and "buried with him through baptism into death." It is important to remember Paul's question: "Or don't you know that all of us [including himself] who were baptized into Christ Jesus were baptized into his death?" As Cottrell points out:

> Every Christian has come within the scope of this sin-destroying force of the death of Christ; we have tapped into its lethal power. When did we do this? In our baptism. There is absolutely no indication that this union with Christ in His death happened as soon as we believed or repented. We did not believe into His death; we did not repent into His death. Paul explicitly says we "have been baptized into His death" (v.3). If this is not plain enough, he repeats the idea in verse 4: "We have been buried with Him *through baptism* into death." (1989:84).

Paul regarded the convert's baptism as the time of entrance into saving union with Christ.

Still, it could be replied that we normally bury people who are already dead, not those who are alive. If baptism is a burial, does this not mean that a convert should be dead to the guilt of sin before being buried in baptism? But as Cottrell points out, "The idea that baptism as a *burial* implies that death has already occurred is an inference that goes contrary to the text itself. Romans 6:4 does not say we are buried in baptism because we have *already* died; it says we are buried through baptism *into* death" (1989:89). Hence, baptism is presented in this passage as the time when a convert enters into death, both the death of Christ and the convert's own death to sin. When the new believer is buried in baptism, the saving union with Christ occurs.

Symbol or Sacrament?

No one could doubt that baptism in Romans 6:1-4 is presented as an act of ritual symbolism. Baptism is clearly seen in this passage as a reenactment or an adumbration of the gospel itself. Romans 6:1-4 is a clear illustration of Flemington's point that "for the earliest disciples baptism in some vivid way connotated and 'symbolized' the Gospel message. It was what might be called an embodiment of the *kerygma*" (1948:49).

But is baptism here more than a symbol? Is it also a sacrament? Nygren does not doubt that baptism is a symbol in Romans 6:1-4, but he goes on to stress that it is more than a symbol:

> It is immediately evident that in these words Paul makes reference to the external form of the rite of baptism. When he who is baptized is immersed in the water, the act signifies burial "with Christ"; and when he again comes up out of the water, that signifies resurrection "with Christ." But it would be an utter misrepresentation if, for that reason, one were to characterize Paul's view of baptism as "symbolical," in the sense in which that word is generally used. For, according to Paul, in baptism we have to do with realities, not merely with symbolical representations. That which baptism symbolizes also actually *happens*, and precisely through baptism. For the very purpose of pointing out this real fact in baptism, Paul uses the forceful words "we have

been united" with Christ, "in a death like his and . . . a resurrection like his" (1949:233).

R.C.H. Lenski agrees and points beyond the symbolism of baptism toward what it is used for as follows:

> Those must revise their estimate of baptism who make it a mere symbol of something else . . . . With διά Paul makes it a means, not only for applying Christ's death and its benefits to us, but equally for our thus getting rid of sin, even of its dominion. No symbol could do that (1961:393).

Cottrell recognizes that it is "the full and unbroken sequence of death, burial, and resurrection" which is pictured here and which is "represented by the single act of baptism" (1989:85). He points us beyond symbol to sacrament with these words:

> Baptism *is* a symbolic representation of a deeper reality, an "outward sign of an inward grace," as the common description goes. This is a truth denied by practically no one. The serious error often connected with this truth, however, is that baptism symbolizes a reality that has *already occurred*. This would be true if we were thinking only of the death, burial, and resurrection *of Jesus*; in this case it does symbolize a past reality. But this is not true with regard to ourselves. In our case Scripture consistently teaches that baptism as the external symbol occurs *simultaneously* with the spiritual reality it is symbolizing. In Romans 6 that reality is the death and burial of our old life of sin and our resurrection to new life. It is a reality that occurs because we are "baptized into Christ" (1989:86).

Thus, Christian baptism in Romans 6:1-4 symbolized a participation in the death, burial, and resurrection of Christ, a saving union with Him who had died for the early believers, an incorporation into Christ and His spiritual body, and a resurrection to a new life in Christ with all the benefits and privileges implied by such relationships. But the force of the language here leads to the conclusion that what is symbolized by baptism God also effects through it. This passage leads to the conclusion that the benefits symbolized by baptism are the benefits God gives through it. Romans 6 presents baptism as the sacrament of conversion, not as a mere symbol of it.

Hence, in Romans 6 Paul not only teaches that baptism had a role in conversion to Christ, but he also teaches that it was the *very time in conversion* when the convert entered into a saving union with Christ. It was the occasion when the convert was incorporated into Christ and when the new believer received the spiritual blessings of forgiveness, redemption, new creature-hood, and salvation which are "in Christ." By using such expressions as "all of *us* who were baptized into Christ" and "*we* were therefore buried with him through baptism" Paul includes himself among those who entered into a saving union with Christ by baptism. If Paul's conversion was complete on the Damascus road prior to his baptism, it was complete prior to his entering into a saving union with Christ. If the conversions of the Roman Christians were complete prior to their baptisms, they were complete prior to their being incorporated into Christ. If we accept this Pauline explanation of the role of baptism in his own life and in the life of the Roman believers, we should regard baptism as an integral part of conversion and not merely as a symbol of conversion complete prior to baptism and without it.

Reclothed with Christ

> You are all sons of God through faith in Christ Jesus, for all of you who were baptized into Christ have clothed your-selves with Christ (Gal 3:26-27).

Context

These verses were not written primarily to explain baptism. Rather, they are part of a letter to young churches in Galatia which had been "called . . . by the grace of Christ" but who were "turning to a different gospel — which is really no gospel at all" (1:6-7). That "different gospel — which is really no gospel" was the attempt to be justified by law keeping (2:15; 3:2,5,10; 5:4). According to Paul, seeking to be saved through law keeping or works righteousness was totally futile (3:10-13; 4:21ff). He even went so far as to write, "You who are trying to be justified by law have been alienated from Christ; you have fallen away from grace" (5:4). Paul rejects circumcision as a condition or requirement for salvation (2:2-5; 5:2-3,11; 6:12-15) and makes the sweeping assertion that "in Christ Jesus neither circumcision nor uncircumcision has any value. The only thing that counts is faith expressing itself through love" (5:6).

It is within this context, a context within which salvation by law keeping and works righteousness is condemned and contrasted to salvation by grace, that Paul emphasizes the importance of baptism by reminding the Galatians, "all of you who were baptized into Christ have been clothed with Christ" (3:27).

Baptized into Christ

This passage is similar to Romans 6:3 in that it teaches that the Galatian believers had been "baptized into Christ." What does this mean? Ernest DeWitt Burton comments on being baptized *into* Christ as follows:

> The preposition εἰς with βαπτίζω signifies (a) literally and spatially "into," followed by the element into which one is plunged: Mark 1:9 cf 1:8a; (b) "unto" in the telic sense, "in order to obtain": Acts 2:38; (c) followed by ὄνομα, "with respect to," specifically, "with mention or confession of": I Corinthians 1:13,15; Matthew 28:19; Acts 18:19; 19:5 (1910:204-205).

Is this view correct? Whatever answer we give, it appears that a proper understanding of "baptized into Christ" turns on the meaning of the Greek preposition εἰς. This preposition is found more than seventeen hundred times in the New Testament (H.E. Dana and J.R. Mantey 1944:103). What does it mean? Does it look forward? Does it mean "motion toward," "entrance into"? Does it look backward, having a causal meaning? Does it mean "because of"? Or, does it mean, not "motion toward" or "because of," but simply what the preposition ἐν (*en*) means, so that it could be translated simply as "location in" or "in relation to"?

As pointed out before, the basic meaning of *eis* indicates "motion toward" or "entrance into" something, including the concepts of goal or purpose (Arndt and Gingrich 1979:228-230). Abbott-Smith defines *eis* as meaning "entrance, direction, limit, *into, unto, to, upon,* towards, *for, among* . . ." (1944:133). Cottrell sums up lexicographical evidence concerning the meaning of *eis* as follows:

> Regarding its actual meaning, a study of the lexicons shows that the primary meaning and the overwhelmingly most common use of *eis* is "motion toward" in any one of a number of senses, the explanation of which takes two full pages in the Arndt and Gingrich lexicon. In this general category the two most common meanings are "moving from one physical place to another" (88 lines in the lexicon) and "goal or purpose" (127 lines—one full page). By contrast only five lines are devoted to the alleged causal use of *eis*. Arndt and Gingrich call this use "controversial" because there is reason to doubt that it ever has this meaning in Greek usage. . . . A meaning similar to that of *en* is not disputed but is still relatively infrequent. Arndt and Gingrich use only 16 lines to explain that *eis* sometimes means "with respect to" or "with reference to." Most of the cases where *eis* is used where *en* would be expected (30 of 34 lines) refer to physical location (1989:58).

Cottrell goes on to point out that "simply counting lines in a lexicon does not decide the meaning of a word in a particular verse," but he adds that such a study does "show that the primary meaning of *eis* involves motion toward or purpose, and that this is how it is used in the overwhelming majority of cases" (1989:59).

Remember, *eis* is found more than seventeen hundred times in the New Testament and Arndt and Gingrich devote only five lines to an alleged causal use, calling it "controversial" and saying "there is reason to doubt that it ever has this meaning in the New Testament." It appears, then, that there is slim evidence to reject the usual forward-looking meaning of *eis*. Hence, *eis* should normally be translated as "into," "unto," "towards," "for," or with some other word that preserves its basic meaning of "motion toward," "entrance into" something, or with such words as "for" which preserve its meaning or "goal or purpose." If *eis* is to be translated as "because of," "with respect to," "with reference to," or in any way different from its normal, basic, forward-looking meaning, the need for such a translation should be quite clear from the context within which the word *eis* is found in the text of the New Testament.

Moreover, Troy Cummings points out:

> The standard English translations of the New Testament should have great authority as to the meaning of the original Greek words. By that it is meant that the combined scholarship of scores of the best Greek scholars, of several generations . . . should surely be thoroughly considered before anyone deviates or goes contrary to their renderings. In the particular point under consideration in this paper, these standard English translations unanimously avoid any translation of εἰς which is causal. Furthermore, they all translate εἰς in Acts 2:38; Romans 6:3,4; Galatians 3:26,27; and in other places as either "unto," or "for" (in the sense of purpose), or "into." Thus, "unto" remission of sins (A.S.V.) and "into" Christ and his death and his body, the church (1957:8).

If the Greek scholars who produced our standard translations had understood *eis* to have had a backward, causal look in the Pauline passages under consideration, it would have been easy for them to have translated them as follows: "Or don't you know that all of us who were baptized *because of* Jesus Christ were baptized *because of* his death? We were therefore buried with him *because of* death" (Rom 6:3-4); or "all of you who were baptized *because of* Christ have been clothed with Christ" (Gal 3:27). Such translations would make sense, and they would flow easily in English. Likewise, if the Greek scholars who produced our standard translations had understood *eis* to have a meaning like *en* in the Pauline passages under consideration, they could easily have translated them as follows: "Or don't you know that all of us who were baptized *with reference to* Christ were baptized *with reference to* his death? We were therefore buried with him *with reference to* death" (Rom 6:3-4); or "all of you who were baptized *with reference to* Christ have clothed yourselves with Christ" (Gal 3:27). Such translations would also make sense and they would flow easily in English. Why, then, were these verses not so translated? Is it not apparent that the scholars did not use "because of" or "with reference to" because such translations would not be true to the basic meaning of *eis* in the New Testament Greek?

This being the case, it is correct to conclude that the meaning of such phrases as "baptized into Christ" do, indeed, have the forward look, the prospective meaning. To be "baptized into Christ" is to be baptized "into," "unto," "towards," or for "entrance into" Christ.

As was true in Romans 6, so it is here: baptism was the time or the point at which new believers came into a saving union with Christ. It was the point at which they were incorporated into Him. It was a part of their conversion. To conclude that they were converted without or before baptism is to conclude that they were converted before they were incorporated into Christ. It is to separate incorporation from conversion in a way they were not separated in the writings of the apostle who wrote to the Galatian believers saying that they had been "baptized into Christ."

Clothed with Christ

When Paul wrote "for all of you who were baptized into Christ have been clothed with Christ," he was using the symbolism of reclothing to represent a spiritual change. As noted before, such vivid imagery was used frequently in the Old Testament. Isaiah urged Jerusalem to "put on your garments of splendor" (Isa 52:1). He pictured the day of restoration and renewal as the day of reclothing with "garments of salvation" and a "robe of righteousness" (Isa 61:10). In the days of Zechariah, an angel told the high priest, Joshua, to "Take off his filthy clothes," adding, "See, I have taken away your sin, and I will put rich garments on you" (Zech 3:3-4). Paul used this symbolism to present the idea that those who were baptized into Christ were reclothed with him. The baptized were now dressed in Christ, not in the "filthy clothes" of their old life of sin. They had stripped off an old life, and they had put on a new one. They had put on Christ.

According to Burton, this "putting on" Christ or "being clothed with" Christ referred to "an act in which one entered into actual relations" (1910:203). Beasley-Murray points out that this agrees with the fact that the antecedent of verse 27 is the phrase, "in Christ," and he goes on to assert that it is

> by faith the Christian shares the sonship of the Christ in whom he lives; he is in Christ because he has put on Christ. This latter idea is evidently a pictorial representation of that union with Christ indicated by the phrase 'in Christ Jesus' and its counterpart 'Christ in me' (Gal. 2.20).
>
> The Christian 'put on' Christ in baptism — the sequence of thought is too close knit to permit of another interpretation: 'All of you who were baptized into Christ did put on Christ' . . . The important feature is that the baptized stripped off an old life and put on a new one (1962:147-149).

The baptized put on Christ in their baptism. They had, therefore, taken off their "filthy clothes" and had been reclothed in "garments of splendor," "garments of salvation," with Christ Himself the ultimate "robe of righteousness."

But what does this say concerning the role of baptism in conversion? New believers put on Christ in their baptism. Baptism was the time when the Galatian Christians had put on Christ. Hence, baptism was a part of their conversion. To conclude that their conversions were complete before they were baptized is to conclude that their conversions were complete before they had put on Christ. Regarding conversion as complete prior to baptism separates putting on Christ and conversion to Him in a way that Pauline theology does not separate them.

Faith and Baptism

In Galatians Paul has emphasized faith as the basic requirement for becoming "Abraham's seed, and heirs according to the promise" (3:29). Because of their "so quickly deserting" the "grace of Christ" and turning to a "gospel — which is really no gospel" (1:6-7), Paul calls them "foolish" and "bewitched" (3:1). Because of their attempts to be saved through law keeping or works righteousness, he asks the trenchant questions, "Did you receive the Spirit by observing the law, or by believing what you heard?" (3:2), and "After beginning with the Spirit, are you now trying to attain your goal by human effort?" (3:3). Paul writes, "Consider Abraham: 'He believed God, and it was credited to him as righteousness.' Understand, then, that those who believe are children of Abraham" (3:6-7). Thus, it is by faith that the Galatians were no longer slaves but sons and heirs (4:1-7).

Actually, Christ Himself was the real seed of Abraham (3:15-17) "to whom the promise referred" (3:19). Christ was the true son and the true heir. But, as Cottrell points out, "Though Christ is the only true son and heir, *anyone* who is 'in Christ Jesus' (3:14) or united with Christ is counted as a part of Christ Himself and therefore as a son and therefore as an heir!" (1989:105). In "Christ Jesus" the Galatians were not only children and heirs of Abraham but they were also even called "sons of God" (3:26). If they belonged to Christ, all other differences made no difference for in Christ there is "neither Jew nor Greek, slave nor free, male nor female" (3:28). All would inherit the Abrahamic promise of salvation by faith. It is all summed up in Paul's statement, "You are all sons of God through faith in Christ Jesus" (3:26).

Where, then, does baptism fit into this depiction of salvation? If God graciously gives His Son so that believers may also become His sons, where does baptism fit in? If salvation is not by "observing the law" (3:2) or by human effort (3:3) but by faith (3:7,26), what role could baptism possibly play in the believer's entrance "into Christ" or the new convert's being "clothed with Christ"? The answer *appears* to be that baptism has no place at all. Surely, *if* baptism is regarded as law keeping or human effort, it *would* be ruled out.

Yet, Paul plainly writes, "You are all sons of God through faith in Christ Jesus, for all of you who were baptized into Christ have clothed yourselves with Christ" (3:26-27). Hence, baptism in Paul's teaching is not excluded, but included. How could this be? Is it not clear that baptism has a significant role in this Pauline description of salvation because baptism is here seen as an expression of faith? Baptism *is faith*. It is *faith expressed*. It is *faith embodied*. Beasley-Murray points out that "if faith is to be taken seriously, so is baptism." He then adds:

> Baptism is the baptism of faith and grace, so that in it faith receives what grace gives. Above all grace gives Christ, for Christ is the fullness of grace; faith therefore receives Christ in baptism. If Paul were pressed to define the relationship of the two statements in vv. 26-27, I cannot see how he could preserve the force of both sentences apart from affirming that baptism is the moment of faith in which the adoption is realized — in the dual sense of effected by God and grasped by man — which is the same as saying that in baptism faith receives the Christ in whom the adoption is effected (1962:151).

Whatever Paul says here about baptism is not a denial that faith is the basic requirement for becoming sons of God. Rather, to say believers are baptized into Christ is to affirm the primary place of faith. Baptism here must be seen as faith, *faith expressed*.

Sinners become sons of God through faith in Christ Jesus. We are saved by faith. But saving faith in Pauline theology is not mere cognitive trust. It is that, and it is much more than that. In Galatians saving faith is faith which "expresses itself" (5:6). Sinners are not merely mental beings, whose minds have cognitive, affective and evaluative dimensions. They are also beings whose composite natures include biochemical, physical, material bodies. In baptism saving faith expresses itself in such a wholistic way as to involve our entire pneumo-psycho-somatic natures, not just the thinking, emotive and volitional aspects of our beings. This is why Paul could write, "You are all sons of God through faith in Christ Jesus, for all of you who were baptized into Christ have clothed yourselves with Christ" (3:26-27).

In view of this, it is clear that baptism was the time when new believers entered into a saving union with Christ. It was a part of their conversion. To conclude otherwise is to conclude that the conversion of new believers was complete before they entered into Christ. The same could also be said concerning Paul's teaching that in baptism believers "have clothed [themselves] with Christ" (3:27). If believers put on Christ in their baptism, baptism was a part of their conversion. To conclude that their conversions were complete before they were baptized separates being clothed with Christ from conversion in a way that Paul did not separate them.

If Paul's insistence that salvation is by faith at first seems to rule out baptism, a closer examination indicates that baptism is included, not as works righteousness, but as faith expressed or embodied. Baptism is the baptism of faith and grace. Baptism is the expression of faith which completes a convert's initial conversion to the Lord. It is the point in conversion at which "faith receives what grace gives" (Beasley-Murray 1962:151).

Buried and Raised with Christ

> In him you were also circumcised, in the putting off of the sinful nature, not with a circumcision done by the hands of men but with the circumcision done by Christ, having been buried with him in baptism and raised with him through your faith in the power of God, who raised him from the dead.
>
> When you were dead in your sins and in the uncircumcision of your sinful nature, God made you alive with Christ. He forgave us all our sins, having canceled the written code, with its regulations, that was against us and that stood opposed to us; he took it away, nailing it to the cross (Col 2:11-14).

Context

The context of these verses is Paul's polemic against "fine-sounding arguments" (2:4) and the "deceptive philosophy, which depends on human tradition and the basic principles of this world rather than on Christ" (2:8). Paul also stresses that the Colossian Christians are free in Christ and not bound by such Jewish rites and ordinances as dietary regulations, festivals, and Sabbath keeping which are "a shadow of the things that were to come" (2:16-17). Since the "reality . . . is found in Christ" (2:17), the Colossian Christians should not return to Jewish regulations which, although they have "an appearance of wisdom, . . . lack any value in restraining sensual indulgence" (2:23). Since "in Christ all the fullness of the Deity lives in bodily form" (2:9), the believers at Colosse should neither be taken captive by Greek philosophy (2:4,8) nor be fettered by Jewish ordinances (2:16-17,23), least of all circumcision, since

> in Christ they have undergone a more radical circumcision than that to which their detractors would persuade them: they have been baptized into the circumcision of Christ on the cross (vv. 11-12). The violent intermingling of figures is imposed by the necessity of controversy, as is indicated by the return to the question of circumcision and Jewish ordi-

nances in the immediately ensuing passage (Beasley-Murray 1962:152).

Paul met a possible cheapening of grace among Roman Christians by reminding them of their own baptisms. In essence, he asked "How can you, the baptized, still live in what you have died to?" The believers in Galatia were turning away from grace and seeking salvation through law keeping and works righteousness. Paul condemned their legalistic tendencies by reminding them that salvation is by faith, a faith which expressed itself lovingly and wholistically in baptism when they had entered into Christ and had been clothed with Him. To combat the Colossian heresy Paul demonstrates the complete sufficiency of Christ, and he points back to baptism, the time when they had been buried into Christ's redemptive action.

Buried in Baptism

There is a close resemblance between Colossians 2:11-14 and Romans 6:1-4. Both passages speak of being buried with Christ in baptism. Romans 6:4 asserts that "we were therefore buried with him through baptism into death" and Colossians 2:12 depicts our "having been buried with him in baptism." The wording is very similar except that Romans uses the Greek preposition διά (*dia*, through) and Colossians uses ἐν (*en*, in). In both passages, however, baptism is a burial *with* Christ. Both passages also present a death to sin (Rom 6:11), although the Colossians passage depicts this reality under the figure of circumcision (2:11). The "circumcision done by Christ" (2:11) in this context refers, not to a removal of a small portion of the flesh, but to the stripping off of the whole sinful nature. The Colossian Christians had stripped off their "sinful nature," had been buried with Christ in baptism and, by the power of God, they had been raised with Christ. By baptism they had related both to the death and to the resurrection of Christ. In Romans the baptized died to sin (6:11) and began to live a "new life"

(6:4). In Colossians the baptized were circumcised of their "sinful nature" (2:11) and God had made them "alive with Christ" (2:13).

As Beasley-Murray recalled,

> The structure of Rom. 6.3-4 was thought to be dependent on the primary elements of the primitive kerygma: 'Christ died . . . was buried, and has been raised' (I Cor. 15.3 f). These elements are even more clearly discernable in our passage . . . Christ's body was stripped off in his death, He was buried, He was raised; in Him the Colossian Christians stripped off their body of flesh, were buried with Him in baptism and were raised with him therein (1962:152-153).

Although in one sense baptism is physical, in a deeper sense, baptism is a spiritual act, a spiritual burial and a spiritual resurrection. Likewise, the circumcision the Colossians underwent was not "done by the hands of men" (2:11). Rather, it was a spiritual circumcision which occurred in baptism when the "sinful" nature was put off. This does not imply, however, that the "flesh" or the "sinful nature" is totally eradicated so that one never sins after his or her baptism. Instead, the concept is similar to Romans 6 where dying (to sin) with Christ means that "our old self was crucified with him so that the body of sin might be done away with" (6:6). Nevertheless, Paul urged those whose "old self" had been "crucified" with Christ "not [to] let sin reign" in their bodies (Rom 6:12). Likewise, in Colossians 3 Paul urged those who had "put off" the "sinful nature" in baptism to "put to death . . . whatever belongs to your earthly nature: sexual immorality, impurity, lust, evil desires and greed, which is idolatry" (Col 3:5). Moreover, he urged them to "rid" themselves of such things as "anger, rage, malice, slander, and filthy language" (Col 3:8). He urged all this upon the baptized believers at Colosse since they had "taken off" their "old self with its practices" and had "put on the new self" (Col 3:9-10). Hence, Paul does not teach that the "sinful nature" is totally eradicated in baptism.

In one sense it is "put off." Yet, in another sense, it must be "put to death" repeatedly as a part of the new life in Christ.

The true spiritual nature of these realities is further emphasized by the fact that the focus of this baptismal passage is on Christ: "in him" the Colossians received their spiritual circumcision (2:11); their spiritual circumcision was "done by Christ" (2:11); the Colossians had "been buried with" Christ in baptism (2:12) and they had been "raised" with Christ by faith in God's power (2:12). Hence, baptism is here presented as a spiritual act, a burial when the old sinful nature was put off, not by human effort, but by the power of Christ Himself.

Raised Up in Baptism

This text depicts baptism not only as a spiritual death to sin but also as a spiritual resurrection. The dramatic spiritual resurrection from the dead which occurs in baptism is emphasized in the following Pauline expressions in this passage: "raised with him" (2:12) and "God made you alive with Christ" (2:13). This, of course, resembles Romans where the baptized so participate in the power and glory of the resurrection of Christ that they are raised to "live a new life" (6:4). Similar Pauline language is found in Ephesians where the believers have been "made . . . alive with Christ" (2:5) and where "God raised us up with Christ" (2:6). Likewise, Paul bases his ethical directives in Colossians 3 and 4 on the fact that the believers had "been raised with Christ" (3:1).

From what death are baptized believers raised in baptism? One death is the death "to sin" (Rom 6:11) or the "putting off of the sinful nature" (Col 2:11). Seen in this light "the old sinful self is alive and well and in control until baptism, in which it is put to death (or circumcised away) and buried, and from which a new self is raised up to take its place" (Cottrell 1989:131). Seen from another perspective, the death from which sinners are raised in baptism is not death *to* sin but death *in* sin. Apparently, Paul has the latter death, death *in* sin, in mind in Ephesians when he says, "You were dead in your trans-gressions and sins" (2:1) and also in this text when he says of their condition before baptism "you were dead in your sins and in the uncircumcision of your sinful nature" (2:13). Seen in this light, sinners are in a state of spiritual death from which they can no more raise themselves than physical corpses can raise themselves from their own physical graves. Sinners are dead in sin. Such spiritually dead persons are baptized, and God's power raises them in baptism and makes them "alive with Christ" (2:13).

This spiritual resurrection happens in baptism. The Revised Standard Version translates Colossians 2:12 as follows: "And you were buried with him in baptism, *in which* you were also raised with him through faith in the working of God." Cottrell comments on the original language as follows: "The expression 'in which' (Greek, ἐν ᾧ, *en ho*) follows in the text immediately after 'in baptism' (ἐν τῷ βαπτίσματι, *en to baptismati*), and as a relative pronoun of the same gender must refer back to bap-tism" (1989:132). The New International Version does not translate *en ho* at all but reads simply: "having been buried with him in baptism and raised with him through your faith in the power of God" (2:12). Although not as clear as the RSV, the NIV still retains the same sense.[2] Not only the burial but also the spiritual resurrection occurs in baptism. "You were buried with him in baptism, *in which* you were also raised with him" (2:12). If a sinner's conversion is complete before his baptism, it appears from this verse that it is complete before he is buried with Christ and raised with Christ.

Faith in the Power of God

There is also a close connection between this passage and Galatians 3:26-27. As Beasley-Murray points out, in both pas-sages

> faith is integrated into the baptismal event. *In baptism* the baptized is raised *through faith*. The divine and human

aspects of the experience of salvation are accorded full recognition. Not that faith effects its own resurrection; faith rejoices in the grace revealed in Christ and directs itself wholly to the God whose almighty power raised Christ from the dead and raises helpless sinners. Marsh, after citing Moffat's translation of this passage commented, 'The tremendous change which these words describe points to an experience whose efficacy can be explained only in one of two ways: it was either intensely magical or it was intensely spiritual' (1962:154-155).

It seems evident that the baptismal experience was not "magical." Rather, it was "intensely spiritual." It was a spiritual experience of faith. In baptism the believers believed, neither in themselves nor in the isolated act of baptism, but in the power of God. As God's power was demonstrated in both the crucifixion and the resurrection of Christ, so the believer demonstrated his or her faith in baptism. Thus, through baptism as faith expressed, the new convert participated in the death and resurrection of Christ. Baptism looks to God's power to perform what he promised. Baptism proclaims the utter helplessness of those who are dead in sins to raise themselves or to save themselves. It looks to the power of God for salvation. Baptism is an act of faith by which the sinner accepts God's saving power through the crucified-resurrected Christ.

Cottrell stresses the importance of faith in baptism and the utter futility of going through the form of baptism without faith as follows:

> When Paul says we are buried and raised with Him *through faith*, this shows that going through the motions of baptism is not a true baptism *unless* the one being baptized has faith in his heart. There is no magical power in the water or in the act itself. Baptism without faith is a futile dipping in water. . . . Without faith the person's spiritual state after baptism is no different from what it was before (1989:133).

For this reason the idea that baptism is efficacious *per se* or that baptism when properly applied brings automatic salvation is ruled out. Baptism is really baptism only when it is also faith, "faith in the power of God" (2:12).

Paul's theology of baptism in Colossians was written within the context of a polemic against "fine-sounding arguments" (2:4) and "shadows" of the "reality" found in Christ (2:17). Since all fullness, all sufficiency was in Christ (2:9), Paul combats captivity by Greek philosophy (2:4,8) and thralldom by Jewish ordinances (2:16-17,23) by pointing the believers back to their baptism.

In baptism they had undergone a radical, spiritual circumcision, a circumcision in which their sinful nature had been put off. In baptism, they had been buried with Christ and raised with him by faith in God's power. By death and resurrection with Christ in baptism, the Colossians who had once been "dead" in sins were made "alive" spiritually. In baptism, their faith was not in the water or in the act of baptism or even in faith itself, but in God. Paul himself summarized his baptismal theology here by writing, "God made you alive with Christ. He forgave us all our sins" (2:13). Whoever, in baptism, had those realities had no need for the "shadows" of Jewish ordinances. Whoever, in baptism, had these solid spiritual realities had no need for "hollow and deceptive philosophy" (2:8). Instead, the new convert had received a spiritual circumcision in Christ (2:11), had been buried with Christ and raised with Christ in baptism (2:12) and had been made alive with Christ (2:13). Paul is therefore saying, "You have no need of shadowy ordinances or of deceptive philosophy. You have the reality, the substance, the fullness. You have been baptized. You have Christ."

Hence, in Colossians 2 Paul teaches that baptism had a role in conversion to Christ. Baptism was the occasion during conversion when the sinful nature was put off and when the convert was buried, raised, and made alive with Christ. To say that the conversions of the Colossians were complete before they were baptized separates being buried and made alive with Christ from conversion in a way that Paul does not separate them.

Summary

For clarity and emphasis I shall summarize in outline form what the studies of this chapter reveal about the role of baptism in Pauline theology of conversion. In Pauline theology of conversion:

(1) Baptism was the point at which new converts entered into saving union with Christ.

(2) Baptism was the time when new converts were incorporated into Christ.

(3) Baptism was the time when new converts died to sin and were raised to live a new life in Christ.

(4) Baptism was the event during which new converts were clothed with Christ. They put Him on in baptism.

(5) Baptism was the ritual during which faith received what grace gave.

(6) Baptism was a profoundly spiritual experience for the convert, not a magical superstitious rite.

(7) Baptism was the sacrament of conversion, not a mere symbol of conversion.

(8) Baptism was an integral part of conversion, not merely symbolic of a conversion experience which was complete without it.

(9) Baptism took place at the beginning of the convert's new life in Christ, not at some later time.

Notes

1. The idea that the believer's union with Christ occurs at the time of the believer's baptism may present a problem to some readers. Can we really pinpoint it that precisely? Is it not like being united in marriage? When does the union actually occur? When the couple say their vows? When they exchange rings? When they are pronounced husband and wife? When the marriage certificate is signed? When the couple is joined in sexual intercourse? Normally, of course, these are all components of getting married in most Western cultures. Becoming husband and wife is a process. During that process, there is culmination in several senses: legal, public, ceremonial, and physical. Nevertheless, we usually regard the sexual consummation as the completion

of the total process. The physical, sexual consummation is so important that in its absence, there can be an annulment, a judgment that a supposed marriage was void from the beginning. In a similar way, conversion to Christ is a process. Repentance, faith, confession, and baptism are important elements in that process. Unless a sinner becomes a penitent, confessing believer, there is no conversion. But, normally, as I understand Pauline theology of conversion, baptism is the completion, the culmination of the process. It is the point at which new converts are incorporated into Christ. Without baptism, conversion is truncated.

2. According to Beasley-Murray the antecedent of ἐν ᾧ in verse eleven is "clearly Christ." But the antecedent of ἐν ᾧ in verse twelve is baptism. His textual and grammatical arguments appear to rule out Christ being the antecedent of "in whom" in verse twelve (*Baptism in the New Testament,* pp. 153, 154).

Chapter VI

THE ROLE OF BAPTISM IN PAUL'S MISSIONARY MINISTRY

If the conclusions listed above are warranted by the evidence upon which they are based, we would expect to find confirmation for them in Paul's missionary ministry. We would expect, for example, to find Paul and his coworkers baptizing new believers. We would expect to find Paul and his missionary teams baptizing believers as a part of their conversion, at the very beginning of their Christian life, as the point of their incorporation into Christ. We would expect to find an urgency connected with the baptism of new converts reminiscent of the urgency in the question and imperative Ananias directed to the penitent believer, Saul, when he asked, "What are you waiting for? Get up, be baptized and wash your sins away, calling on his name" (Acts 22:16).

On the other hand, if Paul and his companions attached little significance or urgency to baptism, such minimizing of the rite would tend to discredit the conclusions listed above. If there were long delays for further instruction or for examination of the motives of candidates for baptism, we would suspect that our conclusions were not valid.

What light does Paul's missionary ministry cast on the conclusions listed above? Does his actual practice tend to confirm these conclusions or to discredit them? Again we shall go to

Acts and to Paul's writings for the only authoritative answers to such questions.

However, before we do, it should be noted that the mere failure of a particular conversion account in Acts to mention baptism would not, of itself, discredit these conclusions. If it did, we would then have to say that the mere failure of *all three* extended narratives of Paul's conversion to mention either faith or repentance discredits the conclusion that Paul believed and repented as part of his conversion. This is, of course, manifest nonsense. Because of his proclaiming in the Damascus synagogues that Jesus was the Son of God (Acts 9:20), we know that he believed and repented. In light of this dramatic action and in light of his subsequent career as a servant of the Lord Jesus Christ, there can be no doubt that, as a part of his conversion, he became a penitent believer. Likewise, we cannot conclude that the mere failure of a conversion narrative to mention whether Paul or some other missionary baptized new believers discredits the conclusions listed above.

However, in this connection, it is interesting to note that baptism is mentioned in case after case in the conversion narratives in Acts. Three thousand were baptized on Pentecost in response to Peter's sermon (Acts 2:41). The Samaritans and the Ethiopian eunuch were baptized after hearing the preaching of Philip (Acts 8:12,26-39). Paul, himself, was baptized (Acts 9:18) as Ananias commanded him to be (Acts 22:16). Peter ordered that Cornelius and his household be baptized (Acts 10:48). These narratives present baptism as the culminating act in these cases of conversion, and they seem to indicate that such was the general practice of the early church.

Likewise, baptism is mentioned in several cases of conversion during the ministry of Paul. From these narratives we can understand the place of baptism in Paul's missionary ministry.

Lydia and Her Household
(Acts 16:13-15)

Following a disagreement between Paul and Barnabas over whether John Mark should accompany them on their second missionary journey, Mark went with Barnabas to Cyprus, and Silas went with Paul through Syria and Cilicia strengthening the churches that had been established during the previous journey (Acts 15:36-41). At Lystra, Paul and Silas met Timothy, a young disciple whose mother was a Jewess and whose father was a Greek. Since Paul wanted to take Timothy with him on the journey, he had him circumcised so as not to offend the Jews (Acts 16:1-3). After the missionary trio, Paul, Silas and Timothy, had traveled among the Syrian and Cilician churches, strengthening them and delivering to them the decisions of the Jerusalem apostles and elders, they traveled through Phrygia and Galatia. Having been forbidden by the Spirit to preach in Asia and in Bithynia, they went to Troas where Paul had his famous vision of a man of Macedonia standing and begging him, "Come over to Macedonia and help us" (Acts 16:4-10). Apparently, it was at Troas that Luke, the author of Acts, joined Paul and his companions, since the "we" passages begin while Paul was in Troas (Acts 16:10). Thus, the missionary trio had now become a quartet.

It was this missionary team (Paul, Silas, Timothy and Luke) who, "probably in A.D. 52" (Ernest F. Scott 1955:3), sailed across the Aegean Sea, to Neapolis in Macedonia, the seaport of Philippi. According to Merrill C. Tenney,

> Philippi lay ten or twelve miles inland up the Gangites River. The city was named for Philip, the father of Alexander the Great, who had founded it as a center for mining the gold and silver that were available nearby. Through it passed the trade that flowed from Neapolis along the great Egnatian highway to its western terminal at Dyrrhachium, the port city on the Adriatic Sea (1961:276).

Luke called Philippi "a Roman colony and the leading city of that district of Macedonia" (Acts 16:12). It was in Philippi that the first convert won on European soil (of which we have a Biblical record) was made by Paul and his companions. It was here that Lydia and her household were taught and were baptized (Acts 16:13-15).

When Paul entered a new city, he usually began his missionary ministry among Jews and in their synagogues (Acts 13:5,14; 14:1; 17:1-2,10; 18:4). But in Philippi there is no mention of a synagogue, which probably indicates that there were less than ten Jewish men in the city, ten being the number required to build a synagogue (Richard Oster 1979:46). But "Jews and Godfearers would often pray by seashore and riverside when having no access to a synagogue" (Oster 1979:46-47). Accordingly, Paul and his team went on the Sabbath outside the city to the River Gangites where they "expected to find a place of prayer" (Acts 16:13). Then, as Lenski pictures it, "The four missionaries, no doubt, introduced themselves, and after their status as teachers had been properly established, they sat down and 'began speaking to the women who were come together'" (1961:655).

One of those listening was Lydia. Since Lydia was "a dealer in purple cloth from the city of Thyatira," Barclay calls her "a wealthy woman and a merchant prince" (1953:133). She was a "worshipper of God" or a proselyte to Judaism. Luke tells us that "the Lord opened her heart to respond to Paul's message" (Acts 16:14). We are not told just how God did this, but "perhaps the method of opening her heart was the preached word" (Oster 1979:47). At any rate, Lydia and her household were so receptive that "she and the members of her household were baptized" and Lydia invited the missionaries into her home (Acts 16:15) since she was now a "believer in the Lord" (Acts 16:16).

As viewed by Van Tate, Lydia and her household were baptized "immediately. There was no delay. There was no requirement to attend catechism class . . . as is often required today" (1987:630). Robert Brow agrees with this assessment and writes, "when Lydia . . . opened her heart to Paul's preaching, she was quickly baptized, with her household" (1981:36). Lenski's view that "We must combine the two duratives 'she kept hearing' and 'to be heeding,' for they imply that Lydia was not converted on that very first Sabbath" (1961:658) may be true, but it is not conclusive since she could have 'kept hearing' for a duration of time on the very Sabbath when she first heard. It appears, instead, that Luke intended to leave the impression that Lydia and her household were baptized after only one gospel message and with no evidence of delay. There appears to be nothing in this case of conversion to discredit the conclusions previously reached. Instead, there is confirmation of previous conclusions as to the significance and urgency of baptism. Lydia and her household were baptized without delays.

The Philippian Jailer and His Family
(Acts 16:25-34)

While Paul, Silas, Timothy and Luke continued their missionary ministry in Philippi, they were involved in an episode of healing (Acts 16:16-24) which led to the conversion of the Philippian jailer and his family (Acts 16:25-34). On their way to the "place of prayer," where the newly established church probably was meeting, the missionary team "were met by a slave girl who had a spirit by which she predicted the future" (Acts 16:16). For many days this unfortunate, possessed girl followed Paul's team shouting, "These men are servants of the Most High God, who are telling you the way to be saved" (Acts 16:17).

Finally, Paul was so troubled by this, troubled perhaps "by the possible link in some people's minds between his message and pagan oracular possession" (Oster 1979:50), that he exorcized the spirit in the name of Christ (Acts 16:18). The girl's owners, realizing that their hope of making money from her condition was gone, accused Paul and Silas before the magistrates and stirred up so much anti-Semitic feeling against them that the crowd joined the attack upon them. Then the magistrates ordered them to be stripped, beaten and thrown into prison (Acts 16:19-23).

When the Philippian jailer received this order, "he put them in the inner cell and fastened their feet in the stocks" (Acts 16:24). Thus, the stage is set for what Oster calls "one of the most vivid and vibrant conversion accounts recorded by Luke" (1979:52).

From the human point of view the setting for this conversion narrative is strange indeed. God's missionaries were in a pitiful condition.

> Besides the physical pain of sitting in a dark dungeon with their backs bleeding from the scourge, and their legs cramped in the stocks, they were racked in mind by a sense of the cruel injustice which they had suffered at the hands of men whom they had come to bless; and their faith was heroic indeed if some painful questioning did not intrude as to why God allowed them to receive such a reward for their faithful service (McGarvey 1892:99-100).

But, whatever their thoughts may have been, they did not respond to their sufferings with bitterness, but with praise: for "about midnight Paul and Silas were praying and singing hymns to God, and the other prisoners were listening to them" (Acts 16:25). Perhaps they sang some of David's Psalms which "have ever been dear to those who suffer, especially also to those who suffer wrong" (Lenski 1961:672-673). This, of course was typical of Paul who "never let imprisonment stop him from witnessing and corresponding with his churches" (Oster 1979:51).

The singing, rather than wailing and lamenting, must have been a strange sound to the ears of the other prisoners who, while they were listening, suddenly felt the rocking of an earthquake which was so violent that it shook the prison's foundations, opened its doors, and loosed everybody's chains (Acts 16:26). As for the jailer himself, he knew that "the Roman law dealt severely with jailors who were unable to produce the prisoners who had been put into their custody. If prisoners who were liable to the death penalty were lost, the jailor himself would be promptly executed in their stead" (Lenski 1961:676). In view of this, the jailer, thinking the prisoners had escaped, was about to kill himself, when Paul shouted, "Don't harm yourself! We are all here!" (Acts 16:28). Hearing this, the jailer "called for lights, rushed in and fell trembling before Paul and Silas. He then brought them out and asked, 'Sirs, what must I do to be saved?'" (Acts 16:30). Oster depicts this scene as follows: "The shock of an earthquake . . . suicidal despair . . . a clamor for lights . . . trembling obeisance . . . and a cry for salvation. This scene is surely one of the most vivid and vibrant conversion accounts recorded by Luke" (1979:52).

We do not know whether the jailer had previously heard Paul and his team proclaiming, "the way to be saved" (Acts 16:17). However that may be, prior events must have convinced him that Paul and Silas were messengers from God who could save him from his pagan environment. On his part, Paul was "quite willing to open the door of salvation to the gaoler who had shut the door of the prison on him" (Barclay 1953: 137). He and Silas replied, "Believe in the Lord Jesus, and you will be saved — you and your household" (Acts 16:31). After this, Luke records the scene as follows:

> Then they spoke the word of the Lord to him and to all the others in his house. At that hour of the night the jailer took them and washed their wounds; then immediately he and all his family were baptized. The jailer brought them into his house and set a meal before them; he was filled with joy because he had come to believe in God — he and his whole family (Acts 16:32-34).

To use the reply, "Believe on the Lord Jesus, and you will be saved," as evidence that baptism had no part in these conversions is to ignore the context in which the reply was made. Paul and Silas were talking to a pagan Roman jailer who had little or, most likely, no previous knowledge of Jesus or His salvation. If what is recorded in verse 31 had been all that was said to him, the jailer might well have answered, "Who is he, sir, . . . that I may believe in him?" (John 9:36). At this point, Paul and Silas had to speak the word of the Lord to him. The following was probably included in the message: some evidence that Jesus of Nazareth was the Lord; teaching about His life and death and resurrection; teaching about forgiveness of sins; and teaching about repentance and baptism. Otherwise, how could he have believed? Why would he have washed their wounds? Why would he have been baptized "immediately," sometime between midnight and daylight? He must have learned these things when "they spoke the word of the Lord to him." The words, "Believe in the Lord Jesus, and you will be saved — you and your household," were but the beginning of what the jailer was taught.

> Those therefore who catch at these words of Paul, and draw the conclusion that salvation is by faith alone, leave the jail too soon. They should remain till they hear all — till they hear Paul tell the man to repent and be baptized; till the design of baptism is explained to him; till he is baptized; till he is found rejoicing greatly immediately after his baptism. It would not require a long delay; for it was all done "the same hour of the night" (McGarvey 1892:103).

Luke wrote that the jailer and all his family were baptized "immediately" (16:33). This presents a problem for the view that baptism should be delayed for further instruction, for examination of motives, or for evidence of deep commitment. The fact that the jailer's baptism occurred "immediately" precludes the possibility that he proved his sincerity and commitment over a period of time or that he was given further instruction beyond the basic proclamation of the gospel. Speaking of the conversions of the jailer and his family, Brow wrote,

> The suddenness of their enrollment [in the school of Christ]
> is still surprising; the whole household is baptized between
> midnight and breakfast! There was certainly no time to
> investigate their character. Nor did it seem necessary to
> check out their good intentions, or obtain assurance that
> they would all persevere in their teaching (1981:36).

In the case of the Philippian jailer and his family, baptism is pictured as important and urgent. It was done without delay, "at that hour of the night," "immediately." Paul did not wait to see whether this "emotional, earthquake repentance" (1981:35), as Brow facetiously describes it, was likely to be permanent. Instead, he went ahead with the baptisms of a pagan Roman jailer and his family the very same night they first heard the gospel. This accords with our previous studies and conclusions.

In this connection, I remember quite well a conversation I had with a teacher in a leading Protestant Theological Seminary in Plateau State, Nigeria. In defense of the probationary model of conversion which would delay baptism for more teaching, examination of motives, and evidence of deep commitment, he said, "But you must remember that in the early days the missionaries were helping our people convert from paganism to Christ. Naturally, there had to be an extensive period of teaching prior to baptism." I then asked, "Wasn't the Philippian jailer a pagan? Why did Paul baptize him the very same night he first taught him about Jesus?" His reply: "That's right. The jailer was a pagan. I'll have to think about that." Yes. It is worthy of thought.

Robert Brow, a contemporary scholar, missionary to India, and rector of Anglican parishes in Canada, is a person who has also considered this topic worthy of thought. Building on the foundational work of Roland Allen and Donald McGavran and after "reading and rereading" his "Greek New Testament, studying every verse that seemed relevant" (1981:8), Brow rejected the probationary model which

holds that baptism is appropriate only for people who have
seriously considered the claims of Jesus, have understood
the principles of the Kingdom of God, and have *proved*
their sincerity and commitment over a period of time.
Candidates for baptism are therefore enrolled as catechumens at the beginning of a probationary period of several
weeks. At the end of the probationary period, the candidate's baptism is a sign or seal that he had understood the
foundational principles of the Christian faith, is now making
a clean break with the past, and intends to live hereafter as a
soldier of Jesus Christ (1981:13).

Brow argues that "there is no trace of a period of probation to
be seen in New Testament baptisms" (1981:17).

Instead, according to Brow, "What is striking about the
early churches described in the book of Acts is that they seemed
to take in anybody! Since all baptisms were immediate, there
was obviously no time . . . to weed out the good from the bad.
. . . there was apparently no attempt made to exclude unsuit-
able candidates" (1981:33,35). Suggesting that "there is no
place for the examiner mentality at the point of baptism," Brow
argues that baptism was to "enroll learners . . . in the school of
Christ" (1981:39).

If anyone objects "but surely faith must be a prerequisite to
baptism," Brow responds in the affirmative. Faith must be a
prerequisite to baptism. But he then asks, with reference to the
Philippian jailer, "how deep could the faith of his family and
slaves be at such short notice?" (1981:37). Brow distinguishes
between "faith to begin" and the doctrine of "justification
by faith." According to Brow, "Justification by faith and an
explanation of how exactly the crucifixion and resurrection of
Christ saved them was taught to those already baptized, as in
the epistles of Paul" (1981:42). Brow also asserts that "the
New Testament teaches justification by faith, not justification
by a decision of faith" (1981:37) and he goes on to argue that
"justification by faith, or living by faith as opposed to trusting
in one's own works, is the main lesson to be learned in the

school of Christ after baptism, and it has to be continually relearned in relation to every temptation throughout our Christian lives" (1981:72). In view of the facts that "justification by faith is not something one can grasp suddenly once for all" and that "Paul had to teach it by letter to the Romans, who had been baptized long before," Brow asks, "How then can we make an intellectual understanding of justification by faith a condition of entering the school of Christ?" (1981:73).

In a similar vein Brow argues that, although repentance is also a prerequisite to baptism, one must not suppose that only a "sackcloth and ashes" or a "breast-beating, self-flagellation, or tearful contrition" type of repentance prepares the candidate for baptism. Instead, he emphasizes that repentance in the sense of *"changing one's mind,* and/or regretting one's past attitudes or actions" is sufficient, and he goes on to suggest that "the repentance connected with Christian baptism is a turning toward God, and in particular a turning *to learn* from him" (1981:48-49).

Brow insists that delaying baptism to examine the candidate's motives or commitment or for further instruction beyond initial saving faith and repentance is to place too much confidence in the candidates themselves. He suggests that the early Christians "had no confidence in the candidates themselves" but that they had "tremendous faith in the transforming power of the Holy Spirit." The emphasis was not on the "good or bad qualities, noble or despicable intentions, sincerity or perversity" of the candidates since they were all viewed as "dead in . . . transgressions and sins" (Eph 2:1). Instead, Brow asserts:

> The whole emphasis was on what *God* was going to do. The Holy Spirit . . . could be relied on to handle the most . . . degraded human material. The school of Christ was viewed as capable of perfecting the very worst of sinners. The suggestion that some who came, or were brought for baptism, were too fickle, sinful, unmotivated, ignorant, or depraved would have been unthinkable. It would have been an insult to Christ to suggest that anyone was too sinful for him to save (1981:42-43).

If this is true, what is the origin of the probationary model? Brow traces it back to the end of the second century and the teaching of Hippolytus (c. AD 170-236).

Burton Scott Easton says that according to Hippolytus, candidates were to be examined with respect to the following: "their reason for embracing the faith" and that "they are competent to hear the word"; "the nature of their life"; whether "if he is the slave of a believer . . . he has his master's permission." Instructions of marital fidelity were to be given to the married and the unmarried were either to marry or to "abstain from impurity." Those "possessed with demons" were "not admitted" even as hearers prior to cleansing.

Inquiry was also to be made about the trades or professions of candidates. Those who worked at numerous occupations were to be rejected. Among the forbidden occupations were the following: "sculptor," "painter," "actor," "charioteer," "gladiator," "anyone connected with . . . gladiatorial exhibitions," "heathen priest or anyone who tends idols," "a harlot," "a magician, an astrologer, a soothsayer." Military occupations were also suspect: "A soldier of the civil authority must be taught not to kill men and to refuse to take an oath; if he is unwilling to comply, he must be rejected. A military commander or civic magistrate that wears the purple must resign or be rejected. If a catechumen or a believer seeks to become a soldier, they must be rejected, for they have despised God."

Beyond this there was an expectation of a protracted period of instruction and/or character development: "Let catechumens spend *three years as hearers of the word.* But if a man is zealous and perseveres well in the work, *it is not the time but his character* that is decisive." Then those who were "to be set apart for baptism" were to be examined: "whether they have lived soberly, whether they have honored the widows, whether they have visited the sick, whether they have been active in well-doing" (Easton 1934:41-49; emphasis mine).[1]

Brow asserts not only that "there is no trace of a period of probation to be seen" in the New Testament but also that many "modern discussions of Christian initiation are flawed by the careless assumption that Hippolytus's model of baptism is a continuation of what early churches practiced. It is in fact a serious perversion" (1981:17). How serious a perversion of what early churches believed and practiced in this regard is quite apparent to the careful student of the place of baptism in Paul's conversion, theology, and mission practice. There is surely no support for the probationary model in the narrative of the conversion of the Philippian jailer and his family. Rather, baptism is depicted as the culmination of these conversions, and it was administered the very night this pagan Roman family first heard the gospel.

Thessalonica, Berea and Athens
(Acts 17:1-34)

Luke's record of Paul's missionary ministries in Thessalonica (Acts 17:1-9), Berea (Acts 17:10-15), and Athens (Acts 17:16-33) makes no mention of baptism. In every one of these cities there was receptivity and resistance to his message, to a greater or lesser extent. In Thessalonica, "some of the Jews were persuaded and joined Paul and Silas, as did a large number of God-fearing Greeks and not a few prominent women" (Acts 17:4). In Berea, "many of the Jews believed, as did also a number of prominent Greek women and many Greek men" (Acts 17:12). In Athens, in the overt presence of the greatest architectural manifestations of Grecian paganism ever constructed, Paul proclaimed the gospel. In response "some of them sneered, but others said, 'We want to hear you again on this subject.' At that, Paul left the Council. A few men became followers of Paul and believed. Among them was Dionysius, a member of the Areopagus, also a woman named Damaris, and a number of others" (Acts 17:32-34).

As pointed out before, the failure of these accounts to mention baptism does not discredit our previous conclusions. If so, we would have to think that the mere failure of *all three* of the narratives of Paul's conversion to mention either faith or repentance discredits the conclusion that Paul believed and repented as part of his conversion. Who could accept such an idea? As a matter of fact, the Acts narrative of Paul's ministry in Thessalonica mentions neither faith, repentance nor baptism. But who could read this narrative within the total Luke-Acts context and doubt that the Thessalonians who "were persuaded and joined Paul and Silas" (Acts 17:4) became penitent, baptized believers? In these cases it appears that all we can conclude from Luke's failure to mention faith, repentance, or baptism in a particular conversion narrative is that Luke failed to mention faith, repentance, or baptism in that particular conversion narrative! Perhaps he did it for the sake of brevity. Perhaps he presumed his readers would understand they were included in every conversion even when not mentioned specifically. But we simply do not know for certain. It seems unreasonable to reach conclusions based on this type of silence, this type of negative evidence. It seems more reasonable to attempt to reach conclusions based on what the narratives actually say in the many conversion narratives which do mention baptism.

The narratives of Paul's missionary ministries in the next two cities, Corinth and Ephesus, however, do mention baptism. Without going into the historical background of these places, we shall concentrate mostly on the place of baptism in these cases of conversion to see what light they shed on our previous conclusions. Will these accounts tend to confirm or falsify our previous conclusions? We shall now turn to another Biblical narrative for further answers.

The Corinthians: Baptism Minimized?
(Acts 18:1-17; 1 Corinthians 1:11-17; 12:13)

Although Paul began his work in Corinth in "weakness and fear, and with much trembling" (1 Cor 2:3), there was much success during the eighteen months he spent there. Among his converts was "Crispus, the synagogue ruler, and his entire household" (Acts 18:8). Speaking of this, McGarvey wrote:

> His conversion, and that of the other Corinthians here mentioned, are not so fully described as those of the eunuch, of Saul, and of Cornelius; yet enough is said to show that the process was the same. "Hearing, they believed and were baptized." To hear the gospel preached, to believe it, and to be baptized, is the whole process briefly expressed (1892:136).

Therefore, this narrative of the missionary ministry of Paul at Corinth accords with our previous studies with respect to baptism. There was such a degree of success in Corinth that "*many of the Corinthians who heard*" Paul "believed and *were baptized*" (Acts 18:8).

However, in his famous protest against divisiveness in the Corinthian church (1 Cor 1:11-17), Paul made statements which, at first glance, may seem contrary to our studies thus far. Isolated from their context, such statements as, "I am thankful I did not baptize any of you except Crispus and Gaius" (14) and "For Christ did not send me to baptize, but to preach the gospel" (17) appear to discredit insights previously reached.

But, it is doubtful that the apostle who formulated the baptismal theology of Romans 6:1-4, Galatians 3:26-27, and Colossians 2:11-14 thought lightly of baptism. Or, as Allen expressed it, "To wrest the passage in the First Epistle to the Corinthians into a depreciation of baptism, in the face of the whole teaching of all the other Epistles, is simply to deny the use of words to convey meaning" (1912:89).

However, even in the immediate context there is no minimizing of the proper place of baptism. Rather, Paul used the meaning of baptism as an argument against the spirit of division. He wrote against the party spirit that prompted them to become unduly loyal to Paul or Apollos or Cephas. Paul rebuked them by a series of rhetorical questions: "Is Christ divided? Was Paul crucified for you? Were you baptized into the name of Paul? (1:13). His answers are implicit. If Christ is not divided, the church, His spiritual body, must not be. If Paul was not crucified for you, you ought not to follow Paul or be Paul's man. Rather, you should be Christ's man. If you were not baptized into the name of Paul, you ought not to wear Paul's name. Rather, you should wear the name of the one into whose name you were baptized. That is, you ought to wear the name of Christ. Instead of discrediting baptism, Paul here implies some of what he made explicit in Romans, Galatians, and Colossians. When the Corinthians were baptized, they were baptized into Christ, into the name of Christ, certainly not into the name of Paul. For this reason Flemington comments, "The passage lends no support to the view that St. Paul is here making light of baptism and depreciating its value. On the contrary, it was just because he had so high a sense of what baptism meant that he regarded with such abhorrence its debasement by Corinthian partizanship" (1948:54).

From these verses we should learn, not that it made no difference *whether* the Corinthians had been baptized, but that Paul did not attach much significance to *who* actually did the baptizing. Perhaps he wished to leave this to his fellow missionaries or to the leaders of the local church. He surely did not want the Christian community to revolve around him or to be built on him (1 Cor 3:11). For this reason he is thankful he did not baptize many of them. If he had, some of them might have claimed that he had baptized into his own name. He wanted to avoid making that impression.

Doubtless, this passage subordinates baptism to the proclamation of the gospel. But that is consistent with the nature of baptism and its relationship to the gospel. Verse seventeen could be paraphrased, "For Christ did not send me (basically or merely) to baptize, but to preach the gospel." It was the proclamation of the gospel that led the Corinthians to want to be baptized. Baptism draws its meaning from the gospel.

Without gospel proclamation, there would be no baptisms. Gospel proclamation came first. Paul was sent for that purpose. But, after the gospel was proclaimed by Paul, "many of the Corinthians who heard him believed and were baptized" (Acts 18:8). Such teaching and practice is consistent with Pauline theology of baptism elsewhere.

Moreover, as Cottrell emphasizes, Paul's use of baptism in these passages presupposes, not its unimportance, but its importance. As he observes,

> In the early church baptism was so important that the human agent who did the baptizing often was made the object of special allegiance rivaling the worship of Christ and leading to factions within the church (see vv. 12-13). This danger was even more acute if the baptizer had an inherent prominence or authority, such as Peter, Paul, or Apollos. Paul is glad he baptized only a few so that the circle of his converts could not use this as a means of setting themselves apart from other Christians (1989:13).

How could Christian baptism have been unimportant if the Corinthian believers attached so much importance to the human agent who had baptized them?

Likewise, minimizing baptism because of this passage disregards the importance accorded to it by Paul's including it within a brief list of spiritual realities that were opposed to division. "Is Christ divided?" If not, His body, the church, must not be divided. "Was Paul crucified for you?" If not, do not follow Paul in a way that gives him undue allegiance. "Were you baptized into the name of Paul?" If not, wear the name of Him into whose name you were baptized. According to Cottrell,

> The point is this: why should Paul bring up the subject of baptism at all, especially in conjunction with the momentous events of the crucifixion of Christ and the potential division of the body of Christ, if it were not among the most vital and serious aspects of the very existence and life of the church? How could he so forcefully and in the same

breath remind them of who was crucified for them and of
the name in which they were baptized, if baptism were not
in some sense worthy of such a conjunction? (1989:14-15).

Baptism here, as in Ephesians 4:4-6 where it is listed with "one
body," "one Spirit," "one hope," "one Lord," "one faith," and
"one God and Father of all," is keeping very good company!
Any attempt to demote or minimize Christian baptism will
have to overlook this very significant fact.

This passage, therefore, and Paul's missionary ministry in
Corinth present nothing contrary to our previous studies. The
teaching and practice here are consistent with other Pauline
teaching and practice on the important role of baptism in the
conversion of these believers.

The Disciples at Ephesus
(Acts 18:24–19:7)

These verses tell the story of "about twelve men" (Acts
19:7) at Ephesus whom Apollos (or someone teaching like
him) baptized, though he knew only the baptism of John (Acts
18:25). Later, when Paul arrived at Ephesus, he found these
men and asked them,

> Did you receive the Holy Spirit when you believed? They
> answered, "No, we have not even heard that there is a Holy
> Spirit." So Paul asked, "Then what baptism did you
> receive?" "John's baptism," they replied. Paul said, "John's
> baptism was a baptism of repentance. He told the people to
> believe in the one coming after him, that is, in Jesus." On
> hearing this, they were baptized into the name of the Lord
> Jesus (Acts 19:2-5).

This is the only case of rebaptism in the New Testament.
When Paul found out that these men did not know about the
Holy Spirit, he asked about their baptism. He takes it for granted
that they had been baptized or as Bruce puts it, "He assumed

they had been baptized (an unbaptized believer is scarcely contemplated in the New Testament) . . . It was an anomaly in his eyes that a baptized person should not have received the Spirit" (1954:363-364). When Paul learns that they had been baptized only with John's baptism — a baptism of expectation, not of fulfillment — he explained that John "told the people to believe in the one coming after him, that is, in Jesus. And hearing this, they were baptized into the name of the Lord Jesus" (Acts 19:4-5). The place of baptism in this narrative is also consistent with our previous findings about the role of baptism in Pauline teaching and practice.

Summary

Accordingly, this study of the role of baptism in the missionary ministry of Paul confirms the insights reached in previous chapters. Paul and his missionary companions baptized new believers. They baptized them without delay and they baptized them as a part of their conversion, at the very beginning of their Christian life.

Whether we are thinking of Lydia and her household (Acts 16:13-15), the Philippian jailer and his family (Acts 16:25-34), the Corinthians (Acts 18:1-17; 1 Cor 1:11-17), or the disciples at Ephesus (Acts 18:24–19:17), Paul and his coworkers baptized believers as part of their conversions to Christ. There were no long delays or examination of the candidates' motives prior to baptism. There is no evidence that Paul or his missionary team postponed baptizing new believers until they determined they really had a "disciple's heart." Instead, baptism was regarded as an urgent matter to be done "immediately" (Acts 16:33), reminding us of the urgency of the word of Ananias to Saul: "And now what are you waiting for? Get up, be baptized and wash your sins away, calling on his name" (Acts 22:16).

We have studied baptism in Paul's conversion, in his theology, and in his missionary ministry. From this multiple perspective there is adequate evidence to affirm that baptism was a part of conversion. Baptism was a deeply spiritual event which occurred at the beginning of new life in Christ and not after delays for any reason. It was the climax of conversion when new believers entered into saving union with Christ, when they put Him on and were incorporated into His church. During baptism new converts died to sin and were raised to live a new life in Christ. Christian baptism was the event during which faith received what grace gave. It was an integral and culminating aspect of conversion, not merely symbolic of a past conversion. Baptism in Paul's conversion, his theology, and in his missionary ministry was the culminating event of conversion. During that sacramental action God granted to converts the benefits symbolized by the ritual.

Notes

1. For many other aspects of this model, including exorcism, see: Burton Scott Easton, *The Apostolic Tradition of Hippolytus* (Cambridge: At the University Press, 1934), pp. 41-49.

Chapter VII

MISSIOLOGICAL IMPLICATIONS AND PRACTICAL PROPOSALS

Preceding chapters of this study have examined various questions and issues which relate to the role of baptism in Pauline theology of conversion. In this final chapter I shall summarize what this investigation has revealed and, based on these understandings, present missiological implications and practical proposals which flow from these findings.

Questions and Issues

Although the topics of this study are admittedly controversial among modern theologians and mission theorists, this work has addressed such questions as the following relative to the role of baptism in Pauline theology of conversion: (1) Was baptism a part of conversion or did conversion come first and baptism later? (2) Was baptism a part of saving faith? (3) If baptism had a place in conversion, what was its role? (4) Was baptism merely symbolic of a previously completed conversion? (5) Was baptism a sacrament? (6) Was baptism merely an external rite which could be delayed for various reasons?

Beyond these questions, a major issue for missiological application is whether baptism should be a part of conversion to Christ today or whether it should be delayed for further instruction, acceptance of a church's creedal statement or for ecclesiastical examination of a candidate's motives.

Conclusions

This investigation into the role of baptism in Pauline theology of conversion has led to a number of conclusions, the most significant of which are as follows:

Baptism Was a Part of Conversion

In Pauline theology, baptism was a part of the conversion process and not merely symbolic of it.

Baptism was an integral part of Paul's own conversion. It was a commanded action, connected with the "washing away" of Paul's sins and done while "calling on the name of the Lord" (Acts 22:16). It was an urgent matter to be done without waiting (Acts 22:16). Paul's baptism was not merely symbolic of his conversion or merely a part of its aftermath. Rather, Paul was brought to penitent faith by his Damascus road encounter with the Risen Lord, and then his conversion was consummated when, three days later, he obeyed the command of Ananias and was baptized (Acts 9:9,19). Paul's baptism was not only something he actually did, but also something he actually did as the culmination of his conversion. "For Paul his baptism completed his conversion" (Beasley-Murray 1966:38).

Baptism was an integral part of the conversions of those early Christians Paul addressed in his "cardinal" passages on the topic. In Romans 6:1-4, Galatians 3:26-27, and Colossians 2:11-14 Paul presented baptism as: (1) the point at which new converts entered into saving union with Christ; (2) the occasion when new converts were incorporated into Christ; (3) the time when new converts died to sin and were raised to new life in Christ; (4) the event during which new converts were clothed with Christ; and (5) the ritual during which faith received what grace gave.

The conversions of the Roman Christians were not complete before they entered into saving union with Christ, before they were incorporated into Him. The conversions of the Galatian Christians were not complete before they entered into Christ, before they were clothed with Him. The conversions of the Colossian Christians were not complete before they died to sin and were raised to new life in Christ. According to Paul, these early Christians received these saving benefits *when they were baptized*. Therefore, the conversions of these early Christians were not culminated at some time prior to their baptisms, but during their baptisms. Beasley-Murray expressed it well when he wrote, "Baptism and conversion are thus inseparables; the one demands the other, for neither is complete without the other" (1962:394) and when he later wrote that in the "primitive apostolic Church baptism was 'conversion-baptism'" (1966:37).

A study of baptism in the missionary ministry of Paul confirms these conclusions. Paul and his coworkers baptized new believers. They baptized them without delay; and they baptized them as a part of their conversions at the very beginning of their new life in Christ. Whether we think of Lydia and her household (Acts 16:13-15), the Philippian jailer and his family (Acts 16:25-34), the Corinthians (Acts 18:1-17; 1 Cor 1:11-17), or the disciples at Ephesus (Acts 18:24–19:17), it is apparent that Paul and his missionary teams baptized new believers as part of their conversions to Christ. As Gilliland expressed it, "The baptism of new converts in Paul's ministry was so much a part of the faith encounter that conversion and baptism could not be separated" (1979:16).

Hence, in Paul's conversion, in his theology, and in his ministry, baptism was a part of conversion. Conversion was a new believer's initial turning to God through Jesus Christ, and baptism was the completion or culmination of that process.

Baptism Was the Sacrament of Conversion

There is no doubt that baptism was depicted in Paul's conversion, theology, and ministry as a beautiful act of ritual symbolism. It was seen as a ritual that reenacted or symbolized the gospel itself. It was "an embodiment of the *kerygma*" (Flemington 1948:49).

But these studies lead to the conclusion that baptism was also a sacrament. It was "an instrument of divine grace" (Baillie 1957:49) which God used as the means or the occasion for bestowing the benefits of being in Christ on penitent believers who were baptized into Him. The benefits symbolized by baptism were the benefits God gave through it. What was symbolized by Christian baptism God gave through it.

This means that baptism was a profoundly spiritual experience for the convert, not a magical rite. The power in baptism came not from the water or the action of baptism *per se*, but from God Himself who chose to accommodate Himself to our composite natures in this way. Baptism looked by faith to God's power and grace for salvation. Baptism was an experience of saving faith by which sinners accepted what God had done for them in Christ, and it was also a sacrament through which God gave the spiritual blessings symbolized by the rite.

Baptism Was Done without Waiting

These studies also lead one to conclude that baptism took place at the beginning of the convert's new life in Christ, not after delays for catechism classes, acceptance of creedal statements, ecclesiastical examination of the candidate's motives or for any other reason.

In Paul's conversion, theology, and ministry baptism was viewed as such an important and urgent matter as to preclude such delays as have been common from the time of Hippolytus until now. The urgent command of Ananias to Paul, "And now what are you waiting for? Get up, be baptized and wash your sins away, calling on his name" (Acts 22:16) rules out any thought of delay. The theology of Paul which depicts baptism as the culmination of conversion excludes postponing it. Without baptism conversion is truncated. Paul's practice in his missionary ministry was to baptize new believers quickly. In the case of Lydia and her household (Acts 16:13-15) there is no evidence of delay. The Philippian jailer and his family (Acts 16:25-34) were baptized "immediately" sometime between midnight and daylight after hearing their first sermon. There was no opportunity for Paul and his companions to prove the sincerity of the commitment of the Philippian jailer and his family or to give them prolonged instruction prior to their baptisms.

Brow was correct when he wrote that "there is no trace of a period of probation to be seen in the New Testament baptisms" (1981:17). In the New Testament generally and in Pauline practice in particular, baptism "was not a 'reward' for attending protracted catechism classes nor did it come at the end of a long testing period; but baptism was a part of the total conversion witness" (Gilliland 1979:16). It took place without waiting, often on the very same day when the initial gospel preaching took place.

Proposals

Certain proposals logically flow from these findings and conclusions. Since this investigation has not been basically an historical study, but rather a study which I have characterized as "theological missiology," it is imperative that recommendations with practical applications be made. Moreover, serious students of Scripture are obligated to go beyond merely explaining the meaning of a certain passage or topic. Stopping there is to truncate their effort. Instead, disciples of Christ everywhere should follow Him more faithfully by using His truth to be set free from sin, error, and human traditions. They should apply the truth of Scripture so as to change and improve their faith and practice.

Accordingly, my intent has been to study the ancient truth about the role of baptism in Pauline theology of conversion and then to apply the missiological implications to the contemporary scene.

Although Paul was a son of his own time, he was much more than that. He was an apostle of Jesus Christ with an authoritative message for Christians of all ages. Speaking of Paul's missionary methods, Allen wrote that he was "more convinced than ever that in the careful examination of his work, above all in the understanding and appreciation of his *principles*, we shall find the solution of most of our present difficulties" and he added that "we must acknowledge" that there is in the work of Paul a "quality of universality" (1912:vii,5). My basic approach in this study has been similar to that of Allen in his classic work, *Missionary Methods: St. Paul's or Ours?*, from which I have just quoted. Allen was presupposing that Paul knew more about mission methods than we do and that modern Christians could learn from Paul. Likewise, I have presumed that Paul knew more about the role of baptism in conversion to Christ than we do and that contemporary Christians can learn from him. In fact, I have presupposed that Paul wrote as an inspired apostle of Christ and that he and Luke and the other writers of the books of the Old and New Testaments were writing by divine inspiration. Their writings are the written word of God, "the only infallible rule of faith and practice."

Based on my findings and conclusions during this study of the role of baptism in Pauline theology of conversion, I offer the following proposals. As the contemporary church engages in its mandated task of world evangelization, it should: restore baptism to its role as the completion of conversion, regard baptism as the sacrament of conversion, and baptize penitent believers without waiting.

Restore Baptism to Its Role as
the Completion of Conversion

In Paul's theology and in his missionary ministry baptism was a part of conversion and not merely symbolic of it. As was the case in his own conversion, so it was in Paul's teaching and ministry. Baptism was the culmination or completion of the process of conversion to Christ. The Anglican bishop from Uganda asked, "Was Paul's conversion complete on the Damascus road, or was it complete when Ananias baptized him?" The correct answer is, "No. Paul's conversion was not complete on the Damascus road. Yes. It was complete when Ananias baptized him." Moreover, the baptism of penitent believers *today* is also the completion of their conversion to Christ. Baptism was the culmination of conversion in Paul's conversion, theology, and missionary ministry. We should restore baptism to its proper role in contemporary ministry.

Instead, many contemporary churches and parachurch organizations not only separate baptism from conversion, but they also substitute other forms or ceremonies in the place of baptism. They substitute an "Altar Call," and they urge new believers to pray the "Sinner's Prayer." As we noted, when Paul was fasting and praying for three days after he saw Jesus on the Damascus road, he was surely praying what today is called, "The Sinner's Prayer." He was surely praying for the Lord to forgive him and to take his sins away. But that was not enough. The "Sinner's Prayer" was good, but it was not enough. Ananias told him to be baptized (Acts 22:16). Likewise, today we should call on new believers to be baptized.

Bercot calls the substitution of the "Altar Call" and the "Sinner's Prayer" in place of baptism "The Evangelical Rite of Passage." He critiques this practice and urges a restoration of baptism as follows:

> Since we feel the need to associate our spiritual rebirth with a fixed day and hour, why don't we tie it to baptism rather than the altar call? Actually, the altar call and associate prayers

are a product of the revival movements of the eighteenth and nineteenth centuries, and they were unknown to any Christians before that time (1989:81-82).

Since the "Altar Call" and being told to pray the "Sinner's Prayer" are modern functional substitutes for baptism, I urge that we restore the original ritual, baptism. This would return us to a practice mandated by Dominical authority and clearly in harmony with Apostolic teaching and practice.

If conversion is "a believer's initial turning to God through Jesus Christ," as I have previously defined it, it is proper to speak of that as a process, and it is also proper to speak of that process as having a completion. With regard to our physical lives, birth completes the birthing process. With regard to our spiritual lives baptism completes the conversion process, the process by which we begin to "live a new life" (Rom 6:4) or the process by which we are "born again . . . born of water and the Spirit" (John 3:3,5), to use the language of the Lord. All that comes afterward, in either case, is the aftermath which follows the completion of the birthing process.

The baptism of penitent believers as the completion of their conversion should be practiced, regardless of the convert's culture. This was true on Pentecost when "Parthians, Medes and Elamites; residents of Mesopotamia, Judea and Cappadocia, Pontus and Asia, Phrygia and Pamphylia, Egypt and parts of Libya near Cyrene; visitors from Rome (both Jews and converts to Judaism); Cretans and Arabs" (Acts 2:9-11) not only heard the apostles speaking to them in their "own native language" (Acts 2:8), but also after hearing and accepting Peter's message "were baptized, and about three thousand were added to their number that day" (Acts 2:41). Apparently, Luke wants us to understand that they were baptized whatever their ethnic background may have been. Luke also records the baptisms of Samaritans (Acts 8:12,16), of an Ethiopian (Acts 8:38), of a Pharisee from Tarsus (Acts 9:18), and of an uncircumcised Roman centurion (Acts 10:48). In Paul's own missionary ministry, as we have seen, a dealer in purple cloth from Thyatira and her household (Acts 16:15), a Roman jailer and his family (Acts 16:33), many of the Corinthians, apparently both "Jews and Greeks" (Acts 18:4,8), and "about twelve men" in Ephesus (Acts 19:5-7) were baptized. Although the new converts in Acts came from widely diverse cultural backgrounds, their conversions culminated in baptism. I urge modern churches and missionary ministries to follow this New Testament and Pauline practice.

As Beasley-Murray expressed it, "there should be a serious endeavour to make baptism integral to *conversion*" (1962:393), for as he later wrote, "In the New Testament, as we have constantly reiterated, baptism is conversion-baptism. Conversion was fulfilled and expressed in baptism" (1966:93). Conversion and baptism belonged together in Pauline theology of conversion. They belong together today. We must not separate them. Instead, we must restore baptism to its role as the completion of conversion.

Regard Baptism as the Sacrament of Conversion

To regard baptism as the sacrament of conversion is not, in my understanding, to take a magical view of the rite. It does not mean that human manipulation has brought supernatural power into the water or the ritual. Rather, it is a "sensible sign" which is "an instrument of divine grace" (Baillie 1957:49). It is the rite God chose through which to bestow the saving benefits which are symbolized by it.

If we regard baptism as the Dominical sacrament of conversion, we are neither free to dispense with it nor to negotiate it in the interest of cross-cultural relevance. The point is not to judge whoever takes another view, but to understand Pauline teaching and practice on this topic and to apply it to the contemporary situation to the best of our ability. In the New Testament generally, and in Pauline theology in particular, baptism has rootage into the redemptive acts of Christ's death, burial and resurrection. For this reason it should be regarded as part of the basic or core human response to the gospel. It is not a negotiable or peripheral matter. Instead, it is part of the core human response to the gospel which should be expected of all people in all places for all time.

To regard baptism as the sacrament of conversion is not to belittle the place of faith in conversion. Rather, baptism should be seen as faith expressed or faith embodied. As Flemington expressed it:

> The truth seems to be that, strange as it may seem to us, New Testament thought could not conceive the idea of any opposition between baptism and faith. The New Testament attitude may be summed up in James Denny's phrase, "baptism and faith are but the outside and inside of the same thing" (1948:116).

Again, baptism should be seen as faith expressed or faith embodied. Baptism is not a work which new converts do to earn salvation. Rather, it is something they do and/or something they permit to be done to them which expresses their faith. Of course, when fallen and lost humans are urged to respond to the "Altar Call" and pray the "Sinner's Prayer," they are urged and persuaded to *do* something. No one would regard either of these modern functional substitutes for baptism as a work of righteousness or as contrary to salvation by faith. Why regard baptism as contrary to faith? Why not regard it as faith, faith expressed? Why not ask sinners to do what Peter and Ananias asked them to do? Why not culminate conversion in baptism, the sacrament of conversion?

Baptism as sacrament involves the whole person. It is a concrete embodiment of a radically different faith, faith in the redemptive death of our Incarnate God. That death involved splinters and nails, physical as well as all the other kinds of suffering. God used these carnal or material means for human redemption. God also uses the carnal elements in *baptism* as a means or occasion for human redemption. It is He, Himself, who meets the new convert in baptism with the gracious action of His saving power.

We must remember that the "power of God for the salvation of everyone who believes" (Rom 1:16) is *God's* power. It is *God's* saving power which saves us. The power unto salvation is not in baptism. Nor is it in the faith or repentance of the sinner who is turning to God through Christ. The gospel is powerful unto salvation because it is *God's* powerful gospel. When Christians sing "There Is Power in the Blood," we do not mean that the physical elements, such as the corpuscles, plasma, and hemoglobin, in the literal blood of Jesus of Nazareth have magical power to save us — if I could only obtain a cup of it, what a powerful Christian I would be. No! Instead, God uses the shedding of the blood of the man Jesus of Nazareth to bring new spiritual life to spiritually dead humanity. Likewise, God uses baptism as a means through which to bestow His saving grace. God is powerful. But He is not a gnostic. He made matter. Since our salvation involves our whole persons, our whole pneumo-psycho-*somatic* beings, it should not surprise us that God uses *material* things as vehicles or instruments of His grace.

We should regard baptism as an act of faith by which sinners accept what God has done for them through Christ, and we should also regard it as the sacrament of conversion through which God gives the benefits symbolized by the rite. Such regard for it will, without denigrating faith, restore baptism to the significant place it had in Pauline theology of conversion.

Baptize Penitent Believers without Waiting

In Paul's conversion, theology, and ministry baptism was viewed as so important and urgent that postponing it was ruled out. Pauline theology of baptism echoes the urgency implicit in the command he heard in Damascus: "And now what are you waiting for? Get up, be baptized and wash your sins away,

194- *Baptism: Why Wait?*

calling on his name" (Acts 22:16). Pauline theology in the
"cardinal" passages presents baptism as the completion of conversion, a view which excludes postponing it. During his missionary ministry Paul and his companions made it their practice
to baptize new believers quickly. Paul and his coworkers did
not postpone baptizing new converts to give them prolonged
instruction or to examine their motives or commitment. I agree
with Brow that "there is no trace of a period of probation to be
seen in New Testament baptism" (1981:17). Although I
understand the pragmatic reasons which have prompted the
habit of postponing baptism from the time of Hippolytus forward, I can only conclude that the case for such delays is more
pragmatic than Biblical. Hence, I recommend that we baptize
those who are turning to God through faith in Jesus Christ
without a period of probation, without waiting.

Of course, if we want sinful people to convert to our creed,
to our church or to our more advanced understandings of the
gospel, more time will be required. In such cases, perhaps only
a systematic theologian or a specialist in ecclesiastical polity can
know for sure when the candidate's knowledge is adequate. If
we really think there must be an ecclesiastical examination of
the candidate's motives to see if he or she is sincere or really
has a "disciple's heart," there must obviously be a fairly extensive period of probation before baptism. But who is adequate
to make such an examination? We should recognize that it is
never possible to understand completely another person's
heart. We can never know, with absolute certainty, whether
another person "really believes, and has fully repented and is
totally committed" (Yeakley 1988:61). We can never totally
understand another person's motives even if we examined those
motives for fifty years. But, if on the other hand, we are merely
leading sinful people to Christ, baptism can occur the very
same day the initial gospel teaching is accepted. For these reasons I recommend that churches and missionary ministries baptize new believers without waiting.

No Concern for Nominalism?

Some might fear that baptizing new believers without waiting will lead to many problems. The serious student might still ask, "Aren't you concerned about the nominalism in many Western churches? Aren't you concerned that many American churches are content to be just pleasant, suburban churches that your average "seeker" can attend (or even belong to!) without it making much difference in his or her life? Aren't you concerned about the extent to which sexual chaos has invaded contemporary churches? Aren't you concerned that the divorce rate among Christians is so high? Doesn't the lack of deep commitment to Christ and his mandate for global evangelization trouble you? Aren't you concerned about the "dumbing down" of corporate worship, the drift toward the entertainment model? Doesn't it concern you that so few Christians are willing to count the cost and pay the price of discipleship? Doesn't poor financial stewardship concern you?" Yes. I am very concerned about these issues. And, I am also concerned about my own personal weaknesses and shortcomings.

However, the solution to the problem of nominalism is not to add legalistic prerequisites to baptism. The answer is not to expect a "disciple's heart" or total commitment *before* baptism. We must not teach new believers to "attain righteousness by themselves in order to receive Christ" (Allen 1912:96-97). Instead, we should baptize repentant believers without waiting. Then, we should begin intensive teaching and training. After "baptizing them in the name of the Father and of the Son and of the Holy Spirit" we should teach the new converts "to obey everything" that Jesus "commanded" (Matt 28:19). As Brow expressed it, "It is unreasonable to require proof of change before the Holy Spirit has had time to penetrate our inner being, surround us with love, fill us with new fruits and gifts" (1981:119-120). But, when believers repent and have been baptized, they "receive the gift of the Holy Spirit" (Acts 2:38). Then we can teach them what it means to bear the "fruit of the

Spirit . . . love, joy, peace, patience, kindness, goodness, faithfulness, gentleness and self-control" (Gal 5:22). Then we can urge them to "grow in the grace and knowledge of our Lord and Savior Jesus Christ" (2 Pet 3:18). Then those whom God has gifted "to prepare God's people for works of service" can teach both the new converts and the older disciples "until we all reach unity in the faith and in the knowledge of the Son of God and become mature, attaining to the whole measure of the fullness of Christ" (Eph 4:11-13). God has great expectations for us. He is calling us much higher than nominalism. He is calling us to be like Himself (1 Pet 1:16). But He doesn't expect us to experience such growth and transformation prior to baptism and without the help of the Holy Spirit.

Proper Questions before Baptism

Another way to view this issue is to ask what question(s) should be asked of a person who has heard the gospel and then desires to be baptized. According to John D. Castelein, "Unless a person consciously and personally can understand his or her guilt and need for forgiveness, and is able to confess that need and faith, and turn from a life of sin to a life of obedient faith, baptism cannot serve the purposes for which God intended it" (1990:2). Precisely! But suppose a person *does* understand his or her guilt and need for forgiveness. Suppose that person *does turn to God* in true repentance because of *faith* in Christ crucified. When such a person desires baptism, we must not ask any question beyond asking whether he or she is willing to make the good confession (1 Tim 6:12-14) of faith in Jesus as the Son of God, the Lord and Savior of all men (Matt 16:16; 1 Tim 4:10). The exact form of the question is not crucial. What is crucial is that the question concerns the faith of the candidate. If the answer is affirmative, baptism should follow without delay.

Asking additional questions at this point hinders the completion of conversion and slows the growth of the church. It is

not proper, at this stage, to ask, "Do you believe on Christ —
and do you promise to stop drinking beer or smoking ciga-
rettes?" In addition to asking whether the person has faith in
Christ, we should at this time ask none of the following questions:

✓ Do you believe in our church polity?

✓ Do you accept our creedal statements?

✓ Do you subscribe to the main points of Calvinism?

✓ Are you a pacifist or a nonpacifist?

✓ What is your marital status?

✓ Do you promise not to work on Sunday?

✓ Do you reject instrumental music in corporate worship?

✓ How should we show respect to our ancestors?

Asking such additional questions when a penitent believer
requests baptism imposes our own advanced understandings
and/or our own legalistic requirements on disciples who should
not have to bear such a "yoke" (Acts 15:10). Asking such additional questions at this stage implies that something other than
becoming a penitent baptized believer is the basis for membership in the body of Christ and for fellowship with other believers. Hence, I propose that we baptize penitent believers without delaying to ask such questions.

Indiscriminate Baptism?

Still, one may wonder whether we should practice "indiscriminate" baptism. Of course not. I remember, for example, proclaiming salvation through Christ crucified to a large group of
Nigerians in an Igbo marketplace. During the discussion which
followed, a young man asked, "If I become a Christian, does it
mean that I must give up drunkenness and adultery?" I replied,
"Yes, the Bible is God's word. It calls drunkenness and adultery
sin. You must repent of these sins, believe on Christ, and be baptized if you want to become a Christian." The Nigerian answered,
"If I can't booze and chase women, I had just as soon be dead!"
That young man was not a candidate for baptism! Neither is a

person who staggers down an aisle at "decision time," obviously intoxicated. Proper motives and the proper condition of the heart are important. As Castelein points out, "This means, then, that baptism should be performed *urgently*, but not *carelessly*. Where people understand, believe, trust, repent, and commit themselves to the new life under the Lordship of Christ, baptism may follow immediately. . . . But where people are hesitant, unclear, reluctant, and have not counted the cost, baptism should not be rushed" (1990:2). Hence, we should avoid careless, rushed, indiscriminate baptisms. We are not attempting to "dunk" as many people as possible.

What I propose (and what was practiced in Paul's missionary ministry) is that we baptize penitent believers without delays for rigorous and often lengthy examination of their motives. We should discriminate enough to know that they are repentant believers. This can be done without lengthy ecclesiastical examinations of the candidates. When we know that the person who desires baptism is a penitent believer, we should baptize him or her without delay.

I agree with Gilliland's conclusion that "withholding baptism from new believers is an unbiblical practice" (1983:91), and I share his sense of disappointment and sadness as I contemplate the following heartbreaking scene from his experience as a young missionary:

> I shall never forget my disappointment as a first-term missionary when, with another missionary and an African pastor, I took a day's journey by foot to a small village church. The purpose of the trip was to examine and to baptize supposedly new Christians. One who was brought in for her baptismal examination was an old woman. She had been coming for three successive years and asking for baptism, but had been refused each time because she could not read the Bible or recite the catechism. On this trip, her fourth attempt, she was refused again. As a recent arrival, I had little to say. Sadly, "knowledge" was given a higher value than faith (1983:15).

Although Gilliland "had little to say" on that day, he has spoken often since then about this unbiblical practice and about the importance of baptism to our understanding of conversion.

What then should we say in response to these issues? Shall we delay the baptism of penitent believers for further instruction, acceptance of our church's creed, examination of the candidate's motives or personal commitment? I say no! To faithful Christians, ministers of the gospel, and missionaries in every culture I address this appeal: When you have proclaimed the gospel and your hearers are led to repentance and faith, do not ask them to recite a church's creed, wait for further instruction, endure examination of their motives or discernment as to the degree of their commitment. Do not ask unnecessary questions or impose legalistic requirements or similar "yokes" which hinder the completion of their conversions. Instead, simply say as Ananias said to Paul, "And now what are you waiting for? Get up, be baptized and wash your sins away, calling on his name" (Acts 22:16).

REFERENCES CITED

Abbott-Smith, G.
  1944   *A Manual Greek Lexicon of the New Testament.* Reprint
         ed. Edinburgh: T. & T. Clark.

Allen, Roland
  1912   *Missionary Methods: St. Paul's or Ours?* London: World
         Dominion Press.

Anderson, Michael
  1985   "Six Pilgrims Share Their Stories." In *Evangelicals on
         the Canterbury Trail: Why Evangelicals Are Attracted
         to the Liturgical Church*, Robert E. Webber, ed.
         Waco, TX: Word Books.

Bauer, Walter, W.F. Arndt and F.W. Gingrich
  1979   *A Greek-English Lexicon of the New Testament and
         Other Early Christian Literature.* 2nd ed. Rev. by
         F.W. Gingrich and F.W. Danker. Chicago: University of
         Chicago Press.

Baillie, Donald M.
  1957   *The Theology of the Sacraments.* New York: Charles
         Scribner's Sons.

Balmforth, H.
  1937   *An Introduction to Pastoral Theology.* London:
         Hodder and Sloughton, Ltd.

Barclay, William
  1953   *The Acts of the Apostles.* Edinburgh: The Saint
         Andrew Press.

  1954   *The Letters to the Galatians and Ephesians.* Edin-
         burgh: The Saint Andrew Press.

  1963   *Turning to God, A Study of Conversion in the Book of
         Acts and Today.* Edinburgh: The Saint Andrew Press.

Barth, Christopher
  1967 "Notes on 'Return' in the Old Testament," *The Ecumenical Review* 19:3:310-312.

Barth, Markus
  1969 "Baptism." In *Interpreter's Dictionary of the Bible*, Keith Crim, ed. Nashville: Abingdon Press.

Beasley-Murray, G.R.
  1962 *Baptism in the New Testament*. Grand Rapids: Eerdmans.

  1966 *Baptism Today and Tomorrow*. New York: St. Martin's Press.

Bercot, David W.
  1989 *Will the Real Heretics Please Stand Up*. Tyler, TX: Scroll Publishing.

Blackwelder, O.F.
  1953 "The Epistle to the Galatians" in *The Interpreter's Bible*. New York: Abingdon Cokesbury Press.

Bousset, W.
  1926 Die Religion des Judentums im spathellenistischen Zeitalter. Trans. in W.F. Flemington, *The New Testament Doctrine of Baptism*. London: S.P.C.K.

Bridge, Donald and David Phypers
  1977 *The Water That Divides: The Baptism Debate*. Downers Grove, IL: InterVarsity.

Bromiley, Geoffrey W.
  1957 *Sacramental Teaching and Practice in the Reformation Churches*. Grand Rapids: Eerdmans.

Brow, Robert
  1981 *"Go Make Learners": A New Model for Discipleship in the Church*. Wheaton, IL: Harold Shaw.

Bruce, F.F.

1954 *Commentary on the Book of Acts.* Grand Rapids: Eerdmans.

1977 "The History of New Testament Study." In *New Testament Interpretation: Essays on Principles and Methods.* I. Howard Marshall, ed. Grand Rapids: Eerdmans.

Burton, Ernest DeWitt

1910 *A Critical and Exegetical Commentary on the Epistle to the Galatians.* New York: Charles Scribner's Sons.

Calvin, John

1975 *Calvin: Institutes of the Christian Religion,* Vol. 2. John T. McNeill, ed. Philadelphia: The Westminster Press.

Castelein, John

1990 "Survey of Key Issues on Baptism." Kansas City: North American Christian Convention, July. Unpublished paper.

Chouinard, Larry

1986 "The History of New Testament Interpretation." In *Biblical Interpretation: Principles and Practice.* F. Furman Kearley, Edward P. Myers and Timothy D. Hadley, eds. Grand Rapids: Baker.

Church of England

1662 *The Book of Common Prayer and Administration of the Sacraments.* Cambridge: The University Press.

Cottrell, Jack

1989 *Baptism: A Biblical Study.* Joplin, MO: College Press.

1990 "The Biblical Consensus: Historical Backgrounds to Reformed Theology." In *Baptism and Remission of Sins: An Historical Perspective,* David W. Fletcher, ed. Joplin, MO: College Press.

Courvoisier, Jaques
  1963   *Zwingli: A Reformed Theologian.* Richmond, VA:
         John Knox Press.

Craig, Clarence T.
  1953   "The First Epistle to the Corinthians," in *The Inter-
         preter's Bible.* New York: Abingdon Cokesbury Press.

Crannell, Philip Wendell
  1952   "Cleanse." In *The International Standard Bible Ency-
         clopaedia,* James Orr, ed. Grand Rapids: Eerdmans.

Cross, F.L., ed.
  1957   "Sacrament." In *The Oxford Dictionary of the Christian
         Church.* London: Oxford University Press.

Cullmann, Oscar
  1950   *Baptism in the New Testament* (English Translation).
         London: SCM Press.

Cummings, James Edwin
  1974   "Paul's Theological Motivation for Mission." Master
         of Theology thesis, Fuller Theological Seminary.

Cummings, Troy
  1957   "A Survey of the Claims for a Causal Meaning of the
         Greek Preposition εἰς in the New Testament." Un-
         published term paper for Bible 24 G3. Los Angeles:
         Pepperdine University.

Dana, H.E. and J.R. Mantey
  1944   *A Manual Grammar of the Greek New Testament.*
         New York: The Macmillan Co.

Daniels, Harold M.
  1995   "Baptism: A Basic Bond of Unity," *Reformed Liturgy
         & Music* 29:2:88-90.

Douglas, Mary
  1970   *Natural Symbols.* London: Barrie and Jenkins, Ltd.

Easton, Burton Scott
   1934   *The Apostolic Tradition of Hippolytus,* trans. into English with Introduction and Notes. Cambridge: At University Press.

Erdman, Charles R.
   1949   *The Acts.* Philadelphia: The Westminster Press.

Eichrodt, Walther
   1967   *Theology of the Old Testament,* Vol. 2. Philadelphia: The Westminster Press.

Eliade, Mircea
   1958   *Patterns in Comparative Religion.* London: Sheed and Ward.

Eller, Vernard
   1972   *In Place of Sacraments: A Study of Baptism and the Lord's Supper.* Grand Rapids: Eerdmans.

Ellis, E. Earle
   1977   "How the New Testament Uses the Old." In *New Testament Interpretation: Essays on Principles and Methods.* I. Howard Marshall, ed. Grand Rapids: Eerdmans.

Even-Shoshan, Abraham.
   1990   *A New Concordance of the Old Testament.* Jerusalem: "Kiryat Sefer" Publishing.

Flemington, W.F.
   1948   *The New Testament Doctrine of Baptism.* London: S.P.C.K.

Fletcher, David W., ed.
   1990   *Baptism and the Remission of Sins.* Joplin, MO: College Press.

Foakes-Jackson, F.J. and Kirsopp Lake
   1979   *The Acts of the Apostles: Volume IV: English Translation and Commentary.* Grand Rapids: Baker.

Fuller Theological Seminary
1986   *Fuller Theological Seminary: Catalog for 1986-87.*
Pasadena: Fuller Theological Seminary.

Gibbs, Edmund
1986   "Conversion," *Theology, News and Notes* 32:2:1.

Gilliland, Dean S.
1979   Class syllabus M511/611 Pauline Theology and the
Mission Church.

1983   *Pauline Theology & Mission Practice.* Grand Rapids:
Baker.

Gilmore, Alex, ed.
1959   "Jewish Antecedents." In *Christian Baptism.* Chicago:
The Judson Press.

Glasser, Arthur F.
1983   *Contemporary Theologies of Mission.* Grand Rapids:
Baker.

Goetzmann, Jurgen
1975   "Conversion." In *The New International Dictionary
of New Testament Theology.* Colin Brown, ed. Grand
Rapids: Zondervan.

Hanks, Patrick, ed.
1979   *Hamlyn Encyclopedic World Dictionary.* London:
Hamlyn Publishing Group.

Hiebert, Paul G.
1986   "Rituals in Modern Life." Unpublished paper.

Holladay, William Lee
1958   *The Root Subh in the Old Testament.* Leiden: E.J.
Brill.

Howard, Thomas
1969   *Chance or the Dance?* Wheaton, IL: Harold Shaw.

1976   *Hallowed Be This House.* Wheaton, IL: Harold Shaw.

1984   *Evangelical Is Not Enough.* Nashville: Thomas Nelson.

Jewett, Paul K.
1978   *Infant Baptism and the Covenant of Grace.* Grand Rapids: Eerdmans.

Kasdorf, Hans
1980   *Christian Conversion in Context.* Scottdale, PA: Herald Press.

Kerr, Hugh Thomson
1944   *The Christian Sacraments: A Source Book for Ministers.* Philadelphia: The Westminster Press.

Kittel, Gerhard, ed.
1932-67   *Theological Dictionary of the New Testament,* Vols. I-IV. (trans. and ed. by G.W. Bromiley, 1964-67). Grand Rapids: Eerdmans.

Kraft, C.H.
1979   *Christianity in Culture: A Study in Dynamic Biblical Theologizing in Cross-Cultural Perspective.* Maryknoll, NY: Orbis Books.

Kraybill, Donald B.
1978   *The Upside-Down Kingdom.* Scottdale, PA: Herald Press.

Kümmel, Werner
1963   *Man in the New Testament.* London: The Epworth Press.

Lacan, Dom Marc-Francois
1978   "Conversion and Grace in the Old Testament." In *Conversion: Perspectives on Personal and Social Transformation,* ed. by Walter E. Conn. New York: Alba House.

Ladd, George E.
1959   *The Gospel of the Kingdom.* Grand Rapids: Eerdmans.

1967 *The New Testament and Criticism*. Grand Rapids: Eerdmans.

1974 *A Theology of the New Testament*. Grand Rapids: Eerdmans.

Lambert, J.E.
1952 "Sacraments." In *The International Standard Bible Encyclopaedia*, James Orr, ed. Grand Rapids: Eerdmans.

Langness, L.L.
1974 *The Study of Culture*. Novato, CA: Chandler & Sharp.

Latourette, Kenneth Scott
1975 *A History of Christianity, Volume I: Beginnings to 1500*. New York: Harper & Row.

Laubach, Fritz
1975 "Conversion." In *The New International Dictionary of New Testament Theology*, Colin Brown, ed. Grand Rapids: Zondervan.

Lenski, R.C.H.
1961 *The Interpretation of the Acts of the Apostles*. Minneapolis, MN: Augsburg.

Lewis, C.S.
1967 "Modern Theology and Biblical Criticism." In *Christian Reflections*. Walter Hooper, ed. Grand Rapids: Eerdmans.

Littel, Franklin H.
1964 *The Origins of Sectarian Protestantism*. New York: The Macmillan Company.

Löffler, Paul
1966 "Conversion to God and Service to Man." A WCC DWME unpublished Study Document on the Biblical Concept of Conversion: London.

Longenecker, Richard
  1971   *The Ministry and Message of Paul.* Grand Rapids: Zondervan.

MacCulloch, J.A.
  1928   "Baptism (Ethnic)." In *Encyclopedia of Religion and Ethics,* 2:367-75, James Hastings, ed. New York: Charles Scribner's Sons.

Machen, J. Gresham
  1947   *The Origin of Paul's Religion.* Grand Rapids: Eerdmans.

Martin, Ralph P.
  1977   "Approaches to New Testament Exegesis." In *New Testament Interpretation: Essays on Principles and Methods.* I. Howard Marshall, ed. Grand Rapids: Eerdmans.

McGarvey, J.W.
  1892   *New Commentary on Acts of Apostles: Volume 2.* Cincinnati: Standard.

McGaughey, Don H.
  1961   "The Problem of Biblical Hermeneutics." *Restoration Quarterly* 4:252,253.

McNicol, Allan J.
  1994   "Baptism Yesterday and Today." *Christian Studies* 14:33-44.

Mueller, H.
  1967   "Baptism (in the Bible)." In *The New Catholic Encyclopedia,* Wm. J. McDonald. New York: McGraw-Hill.

Munn, Nancy
  1973   "Symbolism in a Ritual Context: Aspects of Symbolic Action." In *Handbook of Social and Cultural Anthropology.* Chicago: Rand McNally.

Murray, John
 1959 *The Epistle to the Romans.* Grand Rapids: Eerdmans.

Myers, Edward P.
 1986 *A Study of Baptism in the First Three Centuries.* Ann Arbor, MI: University Microfilms International.

Neill, Stephen
 1978 "Conversion." *Expository Times* 39:7:205-208.

Nygren, Anders
 1949 *Commentary on Romans.* Philadelphia: Mulenberg Press.

Oesterly, W.O.E. and G.H. Box
 1907 *The Religion and Worship of the Synagogue.* New York: Charles Scribner's Sons.

Oster, Richard
 1979 *The Acts of Apostles, Part II.* Austin, TX: Sweet Publishing Company.

Price, D.J.
 1979 "The Protestant Understanding of Conversion and its Implications for Missionary Obedience." Doctor of Missiology dissertation, Fuller Theological Seminary.

Robinson, H. Wheeler
 1942 "Hebrew Sacrifice and Prophetic Symbolism." *The Journal of Theological Studies* 43. Oxford: Clarendon Press.

Sanday, William
 1895 *The Epistle to the Romans.* Edinburgh: T. & T. Clark.

Schürer, Emil
 1979 *The History of the Jewish People in the Age of Jesus Christ.* A new English version revised and edited by Geza Vermes, Fergus Millar, and Matthew Black. Edinburgh: T. & T. Clark.

Scott, Ernest F.

1955 "The Epistle to the Philippians" in *The Interpreter's Bible.* New York: Abingdon Press.

Simpson, E.K.

1954 *The Pastoral Epistles: The Greek Text with Introduction and Commentary.* Grand Rapids: Eerdmans.

Smalley, Stephen

1964a "Conversion in the New Testament." *The Churchman* 78:3:193-210.

1964b "Conversion: What Does It Mean to Be Saved?" *Sojourners* 7:5:10-14.

Stamm, R.T.

1953 "The Epistle to the Galatians." In *The Interpreter's Bible.* New York: Abingdon Cokesbury Press.

Stein, Robert H

1998 "Baptism and Becoming a Christian in the New Testament." *The Southern Baptist Journal of Theology* 2:1:6-17.

Stephens, W.P.

1986 *The Theology of Huldrych Zwingli.* Oxford: Clarendon Press.

Tate, Van

1987 "Acts." In *Commentary on the New Testament in Simple English, Vol. I, Matthew-Acts.* Searcy, AR: Resource Publications.

Tenney, Merrill C.

1961 *New Testament Survey.* Grand Rapids: Eerdmans.

Trinity Evangelical Divinity School.

1998 1998-99 Catalog. Deerfield, IL: Trinity Evangelical Divinity School.

Turner, Victor
   1967   *A Forest of Symbols.* Ithaca, NY: Cornell University
           Press.

Webber, Robert E.
   1985   *Evangelicals on the Canterbury Trail: Why Evangel-*
           icals Are Attracted to the Liturgical Church. Waco,
           TX: Word.

Weiss, Johannes
   1937   *Earliest Christianity. A History of the Period A.D. 30-*
           150. Vol. I. New York: Harper and Brothers.

White, R.E.O.
   1960   *The Biblical Doctrine of Initiation.* Grand Rapids:
           Eerdmans.

Williams, Charles B.
   1952   "Uncleanness." In *The International Standard Bible*
           Encyclopaedia, James Orr, ed. Grand Rapids: Eerd-
           mans.

Yeakley, Flavil R., Jr.
   1988   *The Discipling Dilemma.* Nashville: Gospel Advocate.

INDEX OF BIBLE REFERENCES

INDEX OF NAMES AND TOPICS

Bryant for the clear way he explains our best understanding of baptism to outsiders without succumbing to the extremes of mere symbolism or baptismal regeneration.

John Castelein, Ph.D.
Professor of Contemporary Theology
Lincoln Christian Seminary

Dr. Rees Bryant has properly stressed the close relationship between conversion and baptism and the essential nature of baptism as the culmination point of becoming a Christian. His emphasis and plea is needed for our postmodern era of laxness in doctrinal matters.

Walter D. Zorn, Ph.D.
Professor of Old Testament and Biblical Languages
Lincoln Christian College and Seminary

Rees Bryant provides a healthy emphasis on baptism as the "sacrament of conversion," that is, as an efficacious means of grace through faith. Since evangelical culture focuses on the "sinner's prayer" as the "sacrament of conversion," there is a need to emphasize the role of baptism as the biblical form of the "sinner's prayer." The Pauline understanding of conversion cannot be articulated without also understanding his baptismal theology. Rees draws this connection for us and offers a counterbalance to contemporary evangelicalism.

John Mark Hicks, Ph.D.
Professor of Christian Doctrine
Harding University Graduate School of Religion

About the Author

Rees Bryant is currently Professor of World Missions and Church Growth at Lincoln Christian Seminary in Lincoln, IL. Since August of 1990 he has served as Regional Missions Consultant with FAME based in Columbus, IN.

Rees served as missionary in Nigeria three different periods of time between 1958 and 1984. From 1972 to 1981 he was president of African Christian Hospitals. He has taught Bible at Lubbock Christian University for a total of nine years (between 1963 and 1976) and as adjunct professor at Pepperdine University for six years (between 1976 and 1984).

Dr. Bryant earned his Doctor of Missiology in 1990 and MA in Missions from Fuller Theological Seminary. He received his MA in New Testament and BA in English Literature from Harding University. Brother Rees was the first to graduate from the Mars Hill Bible School.

He has been published in *20th Century Christian*, *Firm Foundation*, and *Power for Today*. In 1983 Rees received the Distinguished Alumnus Award from Harding University College of Arts and Sciences.

Rees's wife, Patti, is the former Patti Mattox, daughter of F.W. Mattox, founding president of Lubbock Christian University. They are active in the ministry of the Global Outreach Team through Jefferson Street Christian Church. As of June, 1999, they have been married 47 years and have 4 children and 12 grandchildren.